**CARMINA
BURANA**

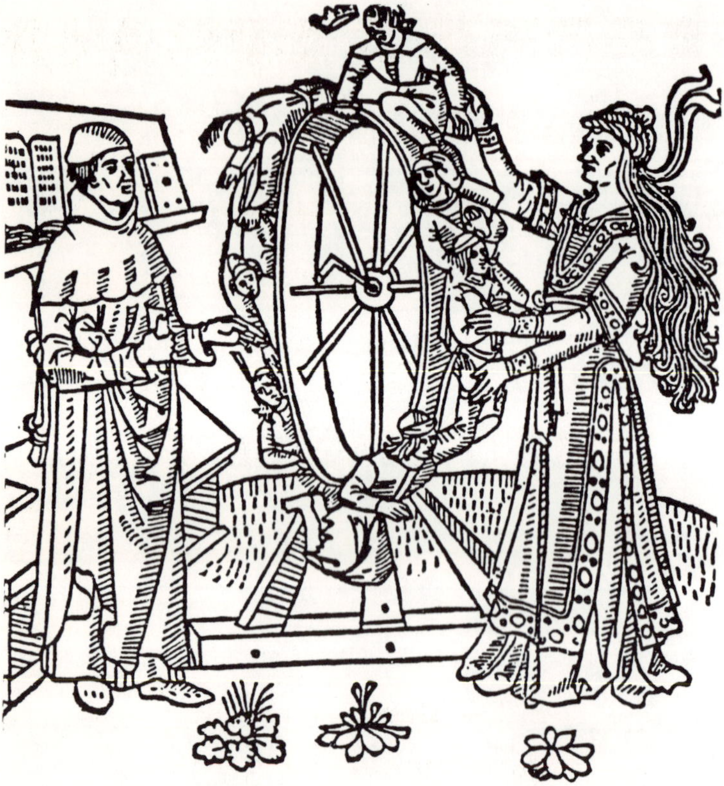

CARL ORFF

CARMINA BURANA
CANTIONES PROFANAE

ORIGINAL TEXT WITH INTRODUCTION,
FACING VOCABULARIES AND STUDY MATERIALS BY
JUDITH LYNN SEBESTA

NEW TRANSLATION BY
JEFFREY M. DUBAN

BOLCHAZY - CARDUCCI PUBLISHERS

This publication was made possible by
PEGASUS LIMITED

Cover by LEON DANILOVICS

© B. Schott's Söhne, Mainz, 1937
© renewed 1965

Used by permission of European American
Music Distributors Corp.,
sole U.S. agent for B. Schott's Söhne.
© Judith Lynn Sebesta, 1983

© **Bolchazy-Carducci Publishers, 1985**

All rights reserved. Printed in the United States of America.
This work may not be transmitted by television or other devices
or processed nor copied, recast, transformed, adapted or utilized
in any manner, in whole or in part, without a license. For
information regarding a license, write:

Bolchazy-Carducci Publishers
8 South Michigan Avenue
Chicago, Illinois 60603, USA

Printed in the United States of America

International Standard Book Number:
Hardbound: 0-86516-033-3   Softbound: 0-86516-049-X
Library of Congress Catalog Number   84-71006

For Chuck and Lorry

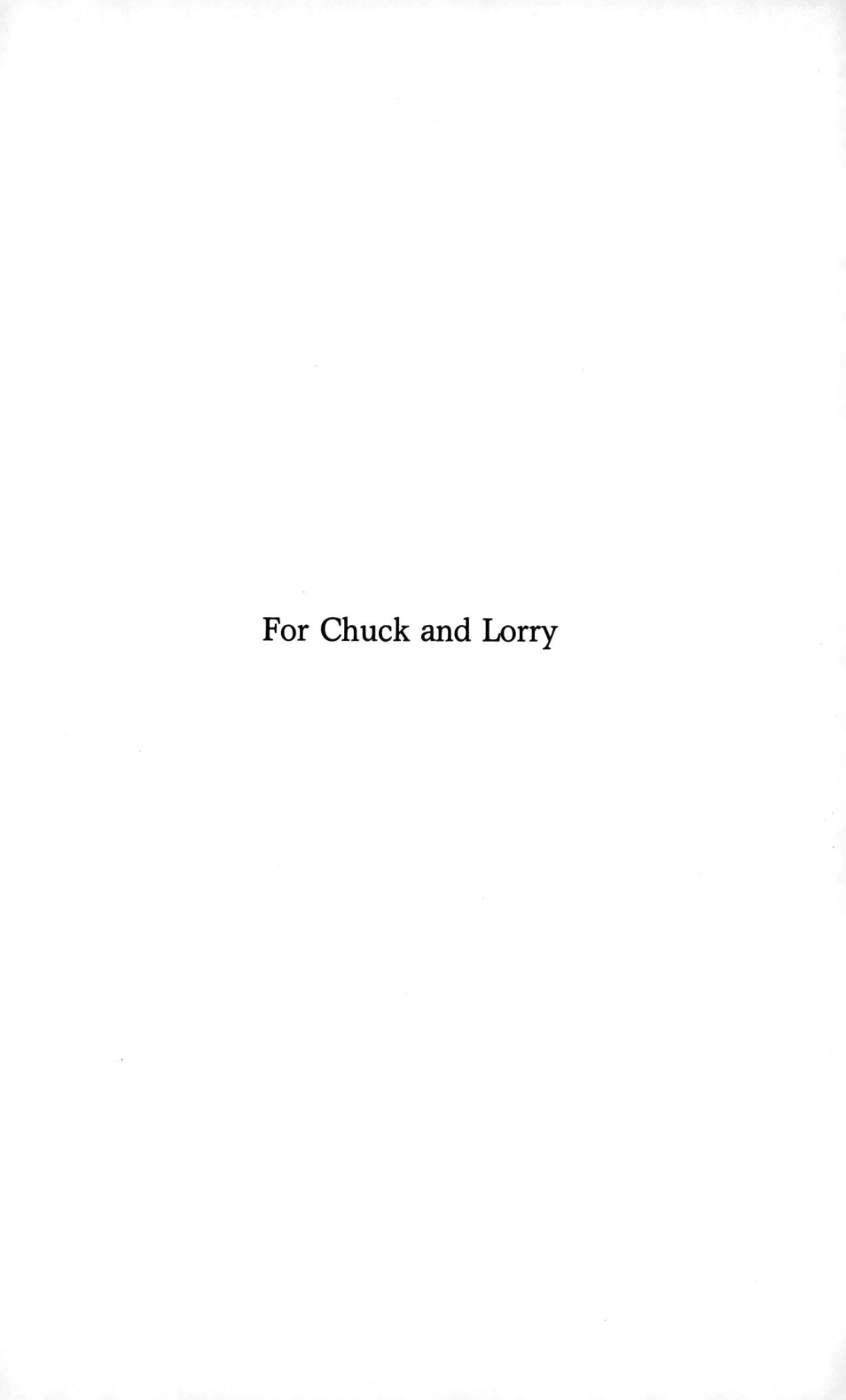

PREFACE

The text contained in this book is the same text Orff selected from Schmeller's edition of the Beuron manuscript (Stuttgart, 1847; Leipzig, 1928) and replicates the orthography and variant readings Orff followed in scoring his music.

In composing the running vocabulary for each *carmen*, I excluded those words contained in Colby's *Latin Word Lists* (1978 ed.) for first and second year Latin; however, if the word in the *carmen* had a meaning quite different from that given by Colby, I did include it in the running vocabulary. All words in all the *carmina* are included in the Vocabulary at the end of this textbook. Starred words in the running vocabulary will appear in subsequent *carmina*, and they will not again be glossed. Students therefore should learn all starred words. Intransitive verbs are indicated in the running vocabulary by the -*um* ending of the fourth principal part. The translation facing each *carmen* is my own and may be used in a discussion on how to critique and evaluate translations.

I am indebted to several people for their advice and assistance in preparing this textbook. First, my thanks go to Gilbert Lawall for his assistance in editing and for his percipient comments and secondly to Jeffrey Duban for his most helpful criticisms. My gratitude also goes to Gale Crouse, James Spaulding and Edward V. George for their shared expertise in medieval studies and languages and to Stephen Metzner for his patient assistance in formatting this textbook on the IBM 370. I owe special thanks to the Latin Classes of 1980-1982 and 1982-1984 whose suggestions and enthusiasm I greatly appreciate. My gratitude goes to Dr. Ladislaus J. Bolchazy for his encouragement and support in the revision of this textbook.

The editor and the publishers, both on their own behalf and on the behalf of students and teachers of Latin, wish to express their appreciation to Mrs. Rhoda Schnur of Pegasus Limited for her generous subsidy given to stimulate greater interest in Living Latin via *Carmina Burana*.

CONTENTS

Medieval Latin Poetry	3
Text and Commentary	
Fortuna Imperatrix Mundi	7
Carmen 1	9
Carmen 2	15
I. Primo Vere	21
Carmen 3	23
Carmen 4	29
Carmen 5	35
Uf dem Anger	41
Carmen 6	43
Carmen 7	43
Carmen 8	45
Carmen 9	47
Carmen 10	47
II. In Taberna	51
Carmen 11	53
Carmen 12	61
Carmen 13	65
Carmen 14	69
III. Cour d'Amour	79
Carmen 15	83
Carmen 16	87
Carmen 17	91
Carmen 18	95
Carmen 19	101
Carmen 20	105
Carmen 21	109
Carmen 22	113
Carmen 23	119
Carmen 24	123
Fortuna Imperatrix Mundi	
Carmen 25	126
Fortuna Imperatrix Mundi	129
Carl Orff	137
Medieval Latin	139
Recordings	141
Bibliography	142
Vocabulary	143
Duban's Translation	157

ILLUSTRATIONS

The Wheel of Fortune	iv
Rose of Learning	12
Hecuba Enslaved	17
Simus iussi Cypridis	18
Spring Plowing	25
Flora	26
Phoebus	38
Peasants Dancing	48
Ad ludum properamus	56
In the Devil's Kitchen	66
Cupid (as Devil) with lovers in a garden	81
Cupid	84
Stetit puella	88
Maiden, young men, Cupid	98
Youth and Maiden	102
Goliard	106
The Dance of Death	116
Fortuna from the Beuron ms.	125

Acknowledgments

Acknowledgments for use of the above illustrations are made to: the British Museum; Dover Publications; Harvard University Press.

MEDIEVAL LATIN POETRY

TEXT AND COMMENTARY

MEDIEVAL LATIN POETRY

The medieval Latin poetry in the collection known as the *Carmina Burana* is very unlike the poetry of Catullus or Vergil which uses Greek quantitative patterns of long and short syllables. It resembles, rather, the very early Latin poetry which was accentual and stressed. This native Latin poetry, called Saturnian, did not disappear entirely after Greek versification became the style in 240 B.C. Soldiers on the march sang songs in Saturnian verse, as did street musicians, the patrons of the local tavern, and children at play.

Since Christianity was, at first, a religion primarily of the *vulgus* or common people, it is not surprising that the earliest Christian hymns written in Latin were accentual rather than quantitative. Commodian, the earliest extant Christian writer of Latin verse, was popular with congregations of the third century because he wrote his hymns in the accentual verse with which they were familiar. Moreover, his verse contains another characteristic of medieval Latin poetry which lends charm to his words, namely rhyme.

> Namque fatebor enim unum me ex vobis adesse
> Terroremque item quondam sensisse ruinae.
> Idcirco commoneo vulneratos cautius ire,
> Barbam (atque) comam foedare in pulvere terrae
> Volutarique saccis et petere summo de Rege
> Subvenire tibi, ne pereas forte de plebe.
> *(Instr. II viii)*

MEDIEVAL LATIN POETRY

Constantine's Edict of Milan (A.D. 313) allowed Christian worship to be conducted publicly, and, in the years following, Christians of the West used, more and more, Latin (rather than Greek) as the language of their liturgy. They translated Greek hymns into Latin and composed new Latin ones. The most skilled and popular composers were St. Ambrose, Prudentius, and Venantius Fortunatus. Many of their hymns, now translated into English, are sung in American churches of every denomination today.

The poems in the *Carmina Burana* are secular, and yet some of them resemble hymns, as Orff's musical arrangement clearly points out. This resemblance is due to the ecclesiastical background of their composers, a group of poets known as the Goliards.

The twelfth century, the period of the Goliards, was a period of intellectual and cultural ferment. This century saw universities established with students swarming to them, hopeful of rising in status through entry into one of the professions or the church. New literature was written as the classical epic of Vergil was adapted to the recounting of the adventures of King Arthur, Roland, Tristam and Iseult in the vernacular languages. Nonetheless, Latin was a living language for the people of the twelfth century. Latin was the language used to argue cases in law courts, to present petitions to the king, to write contracts in business offices, to give lectures in universities, and to praise one's beloved in the quiet of a garden. Though the Goliards used the language of Vergil, they drew their topics from the hum of busy medieval life around them. They bridged two worlds, the classical and the contemporary.

The origin of the name "Goliard" given to them is unclear. Some contemporaries thought it came from *gula* (gluttony), since Goliards enjoyed drinking and eating. A more erudite, but scarcely more flattering, etymology was that they were named after Goliath, called Golias in the Latin of the Vulgate. Goliath or Golias was a giant, a monster, an agent of the Devil against the Israelites and he seemed an appropriate hero for the bawdy and irreverent poets. So the strict and pious Abbess Herrad von Landsberg thought, and in an illustration in her erudite *Hortus Deliciarum*, written to improve her nuns' minds, she shows these secular poets listening intently to the whispers of the Devil as they compose their next song of debauchery.

"Goliard" was a general name given to any street poet living by his wits. Usually he had been at one time a monk in a quiet cloister dedicated

MEDIEVAL LATIN POETRY

to a pious life of spiritual, not sensual devotion. Or perhaps he had been a student, seriously committed to study with the hope of advancing in one of the professions or of entering the church at a high level. But now he lived a life of chance and danger, using his wits to support himself. A few lucky Goliards gained a more secure life by being adopted by some rich patron, just as the Archpoet, the most famous Goliard, had himself been taken up by the Archbishop of Cologne. Most Goliards roved from town to town, begging food and lodging, earning some coins by pleasing their audience with their songs. In taverns, drinking songs were demanded or perhaps satiric songs about rapacious clergy whom everyone had to pay annually a full tenth of their income, good harvest or no. In the home of a merchant or someone of high social standing, the poet might sing a song of love or one of more philosophical bent.

Why had the monk deserted his cloister and the student the university for a life more frequently unpleasant and dangerous than the reverse? The songs of the Goliards speak of disillusionment with the world. The monk heard sermons praising poverty and good works--and saw money buying high positions in the church. Faced with intense competition the student despaired of ever gaining entrance into one of the professions. Many Goliards were drop-outs of medieval society. They expressed their disappointment in songs of burning anger, such as *carmen* 11, and of savage satire and parody such as *carmen* 13 and 14. They did worse. Church ceremonies and hymns were mocked in their poems, slyly or openly. The hymn to the Virgin Mary, *"Verbum bonum et suave,"* was parodied as a hymn in praise of wine, *"Vinum bonum et suave."* The Mass was even parodied, where *bibamus* replaced *oremus* and the benediction was "Fraud be with you." As you translate the *carmina* in Orff's selection, keep in mind the ecclesiastical background of many of the Goliardic poets and compare the poets' philosophy and ideas of love and life to the ideals and principles of the church and society against which they were revolting.

Medieval Latin verse differs from classical Latin verse in two important respects. Unlike classical Latin poetry which insisted on strict observance of quantitative metrical patterns, medieval Latin poetry used a more or less regular pattern of stressed and unstressed syllables in a line of poetry. Goliards, however, were particularly fond of trochaic tetrameter, a meter superbly illustrated by *carmen* 11 in this textbook, and consequently this meter is frequently called "Goliardic." Another feature of medieval Latin verse, not found in classical Latin verse, is the repetition of identical or similar sounds, at the end of the verse, called end-rhyme or terminal-rhyme. Such rhyme is attractive *per se* to the ear and adds much charm to the poem.

Sometime in the late thirteenth century or soon thereafter, a Benedictine monk at the monastery of Beuron in Bavaria collected about 200 Goliardic poems into an anthology now known as the *Carmina Burana*. Containing mostly the poems of French and German Goliards, this collection ranges in quality from the sublime to the paltry. The poets sing of the crusades, castigate corrupt practices of the church, beg for food, and their previous vows notwithstanding, court maidens and praise the delights of love and spring. Necessarily kept hidden, the anthology remained at Beuron until the monastery was dissolved. The manuscript was brought to Munich and published by Schmeller in 1847. Out of this anthology Carl Orff selected certain *carmina* composed in Latin, or Latin mixed with French and German, which he set to music in 1937.

FORTUNA IMPERATRIX MUNDI

CARMEN 1
CARMEN 2

Carmen 1 is repeated at the end of Orff's selected arrangement of *Carmina Burana* as *carmen* 25. Fortuna is the theme of this *carmen*, with whom each of the other *carmina* is connected. Since she is *imperatrix mundi*, as Orff calls her, these other *carmina* reveal, in one way or another, her actions in the world. Indeed, the Beuron manuscript contains a picture of the wheel of Fortuna which is inscribed with the words in lines 17-20 of *carmen* 2. These words, in a sense, become the motto for the whole collection.

A full chorus sings *carmen* 1. Orff's solemn arrangement for massed voices brings out the hymnlike quality of this *carmen* and equates it with such full choruses as those in Handel's *Messiah*. There is, however, a major difference between such an arrangement of Handel's and Orff's arrangement. Orff's chorus sings in harmonic unison; his arrangement, a chorale, has no counterpoint or elaborate harmony and is more akin to the "plain song" of the early Christian hymns, such as the Gregorian chant.

Carmen 1 extolls Fortuna's power, while *carmen* 2 gives an example of her power in action. Written in the first person, *carmen* 2 is personal, yet it is sung also by the full chorus.

In *carmina* 1 and 2 Fortuna is described as controlling a wheel, a symbol of her action in the world which can be seen today in any gambling casino.

VOCABULARY

    imperātrix, -icis F.: she who rules; empress

    ***mundus, -ī** M.: the world and its inhabitants

2 **velut** (adverb). just as, as (often used to introduce comparisons)

3 **status, -ūs** M. state, condition. Statū is ablative of respect.

    variābilis, -e. varying, variable, changeable

4 **crescō, 3, crēvī, crētum.** to grow, increase, wax

5 ***dēcrescō, 3, -crēvī, -crētum.** to grow smaller, decrease, wane

6 **dētestābilis, -e.** abominable, execrable, detestable

7 **obdūrō, 1.** to harden, render hard

8 **tunc** (adverb). then

    cūrō, 1. to take care of, tend, treat; pamper

9 ***lūdus, -ī** M. game, sport; pastime; joke. Lūdō is ablative of means construed with obdurat and curat, and refers to the capricious ups and downs of good and bad fortune.

    aciēs, -ēī F. acuteness, sharpness; power

10 **egestās, -ātis** F. poverty, want

11 **potestās, -ātis** F. prosperity

12 **dissolvō, 3, -solvī, -solūtus.** to loosen, separate; destroy

    ***ut** (adverb). as, just as (used to introduce comparisons)

    glaciēs, -ēī F. ice
      The understood expression of lines 10-12 is: vīta (line 6) egestātem et potestātem dissolvit ut sōl glaciem dissolvit.

13 ***sors, sortis** F. a lot, or that which is used in selection by chance, such as a slip of paper drawn from a container; fortune, fate

    immānis, -e. monstrous; savage, horrible, inhuman

14 **inānis, -e.** void, empty; unprofitable, worthless

15 ***rota, -ae** F. wheel. Rota, salūs, status are all in apposition to sors.

    volūbilis, -e. spinning, revolving, turning

16 **malus, -a, -um.** bad, evil

17 ***vānus, -a, -um.** empty, void; vain; unreliable, untrue

    salus, salūtis F. health, safety, welfare; prosperity

1. O FORTUNA

Ō Fortūna
  velut lūna
    statū variābilis,
      semper crescis
        aut dēcrescis;   5
vīta dētestābilis
  nunc obdūrat
    et tunc cūrat
lūdō mentis aciem;
  egestātem,   10
  potestātem
dissolvit ut glaciem.

  Sors immānis,
    et inānis
rota tu volūbilis,   15
  status malus,
    vāna salūs

O Fortune, like the moon
you are always changing,
waxing now, now waning,
never the same for long remaining.
How can we love this hateful life
which pampers us, then harries us,
bemusing and confusing us,
always in temper humorous—
poverty, prosperity,
dissolving both as sun does ice?

O Luck, ill of nature, ill of will,
you spin us round at dizzy rate,
carrying us to high estate,
then to ruin, your heart obdurate.
Your profitless prosperity like mist

VOCABULARY, continued

18 **dissolūbilis, -e.** dissolvable, destroyable
19 **obumbrātus, -a, -um.** covered up, wrapped, enveloped
20 **vēlātus, -a, -um.** veiled, covered up, hidden
21 **michi** (medieval Latin form): **mihi**
   nītor, 3, nīsus (nixus). to press forward, to labor; to attack (+ dative)
23 **dorsum, -ī** N. back
24 **scelus, sceleris** N. misfortune resulting from the ill will of the gods; an affliction, curse
   Lines 22-24 should be construed thus: nunc per lūdum tuī sceleris dorsum meum nūdum ferō.
26 *****virtūs, -tūtis** F. virtue; salvation
27 *****contrārius, -a, -um.** contrary, opposed (+ dative)
28 **affectus, -ūs** M. eagerness, zeal; attention
29 **dēfectus, -ūs** M. failure; absence
30 **angāria, -ae** F. forced service; tribulation; struggle
   The sense of lines 25-30 is: sors (fortūna) salūtis et virtūtis mihi nunc contrāria est; est affectus (sortis) et est dēfectus (sortis) semper in angāriā.
33 *****cor, cordis** N. heart, feeling. Corde is ablative of place without a preposition.
   pulsus, -ūs M. beat, throb, stroke; beating of heart, pulse
35 **sternō, 3, strāvī, strātus.** to scatter, overthrow
36 *****plangō, 3, planxī, planctus.** to lament, beat one's breast, bewail.
   The sense of lines 34-36 is: omnēs mēcum plangite quod, per sortem, fortūna mē, fortem virum, sternit.

1. O FORTUNA, *continued*

semper dissolūbilis,
   obumbrāta
   et vēlāta   20
michi quoque nīteris
   nunc per lūdum
   dorsum nūdum
ferō tuī sceleris.

   Sors salūtis   25
   et virtūtis
michi nunc contrāria;
   est affectus
   et dēfectus
semper in angāriā.   30
   Hāc in hōrā
   sine morā
corde pulsum tangite;
   quod per sortem
   sternit fortem   35
mēcum omnēs plangite.

dissolving, then again us involving,
future veiling, us assailing,
grace and salvation denying.
   To Fortune's blows
I bare my back.

O Luck, you ruin my health and strength,
robbing me of all confidence;
I bless your presence,
curse your absence,
living my life in painful hesitance.
Let us all mourn together
For in this very hour
Fortune shows her power!
   Fortune in her whimsy
overwhelms the brave.

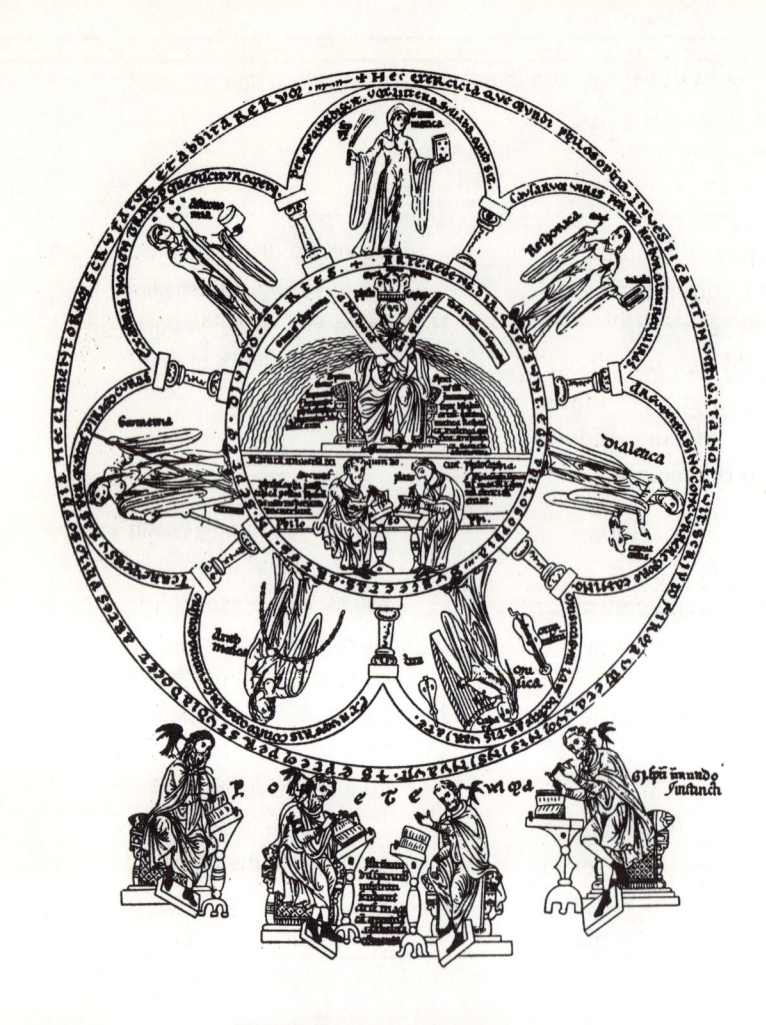

THE ROSE OF LEARNING

Through this illustration, mentioned on page 4, the Abbess Herrad showed her disapproval of the poetry Goliards wrote. The rose window, developed from the round windows of Roman imperial buildings, became a distinguishing feature of Gothic cathedrals, usually decorating the west end of the nave or the ends of the transepts. Stone bars outlined the "petals". In this drawing, Philosophy sits, crowned, in the center; at her feet are Socrates and Plato. In the petals are figures representing the Seven Liberal Arts. Going clockwise from the top are Grammar, Rhetoric, and Dialectic which formed the curriculum of the Trivium; then come Music, Arithmetic, Geometry, and Astronomy, which formed the curriculum of the Quadrivium. Outside the closed Circle of Knowledge are poets and intellectuals at their writing desks, intently listening to the lies and ungodly suggestions of the ravens, which are the Devil's emissaries. (Illustration from G. Whicher, *The Goliard Poets;* see Bibliography.)

While not overly difficult grammatically, *carmen* 1 does pose some problems for the modern translator because the poet is often expressing two ideas in the words of a single sentence. It may be possible for you in translating to be as skilled in your poetry, but you should feel free to paraphrase, or "spell out," more clearly the poet's double meanings, rather than trying a "word for word" translation.

An example of this "compression" of ideas occurs in lines 6-8, where *vita* replaces *Fortuna*. Here we have an example of metonymy, a figure of speech in which one word is substituted for another to which the word is closely connected in thought; thus one may speak of the "scepter of England," while meaning the queen of England. In these lines, the poet replaces *Fortuna* with *vita,* since Fortuna "toys" with man's life. What does the poet mean by *acies mentis?* Literally, the phrase means "the keenness of the mind." By "keenness" does the poet mean "intelligence"? Consider our English expressions, "a mind dulled by care," "a mind sharpened by anxiety." To what quality or aspect of the mind do these phrases refer? Is this quality what the poet means by *acies?* Can you find a single word to translate *acies* or must you paraphrase and "spell out" in several words the poet's meaning? Note that *ludo* is repeated in lines 9 and 22. Can you translate these two occurrences by the same English word or will you have to paraphrase one or both?

In lines 13-14 the poet calls *sors* both *immanis* and *inanis.* Both words describe *Fortuna* in relation to the effect she has on this life. Are these two words appropriate descriptions of *Fortuna?* In what way(s) is she both *immanis* and *inanis?*

Another passage better rendered by paraphrase than by literal translation occurs in lines 28-30. Before attempting a paraphrase you should consider the feudal background of the Goliards. What picture of the relationship between the poet and *Fortuna* does the word *angaria* give?

You may wish to paraphrase line 33 also: *(in) corde (mea) pulsum tangite.* Does your paraphrase, or a more literal translation, bring out more emphatically the poet's plea? Lines 31-36 are addressed to a wider audience than the rest of the poem which up to this point has been a soliloquy. Why does the poet suddenly address us? How does this change in form from soliloquy to direct address change the tone of the poem? As you read *carmen* 2, note whether the poet again enlarges his audience from himself to all of us.

13

VOCABULARY

       Fortūnē (medieval Latin form): **Fortūnae**
2   **stillō,** 1. to drop, trickle, drip
       ocellus, -ī M.. eye (The diminutive forms connotes endearment, e.g. "my own dear eyes").
4   **subtrahō,** 3, **-traxī, -tractus.** to take away, remove
       rebellis, -e. always making war
5   *****legō,** 3, **lēgī, lectus.** to read
6   **capillātus, -a, -um.** having long hair
7   **sequor,** 3, **secūtus.** to come
8   **Occāsiō, -ōnis** F. Opportunity, Chance
       calvātus, -a, -um. bald
       The sense of lines 5-8 is: id quod legitur vērum est--capillāta est, sed plērumque calvāta sequitur.
9   **solium, -ī** N. throne
10   **sedeō,** 2, **sedī, sessum.** to sit
       ēlātus, -a, -um. exalted, lofty, high
11   **prosperitās, -ātis** F. prosperity, riches
       *****varius, -a, -um.** colorful
12   *****flōs, flōris** M. flower
       corōnātus, -a, -um. crowned
13   *****quisquis, quaequae, quicquid.** whoever, whatever.
       (In line 13 quisquid is the contracted form of quibusquid, a dative of reference.).
       *****flōreō,** 2, **flōruī,** ----. to bloom, blossom, flourish
14   *****fēlix, fēlicis.** happy, lucky, prosperous
       beātus, -a, -um. happy, blessed, fortunate
15   **summum, -ī** N. highest point, top
       corruō, 3, **corruī,** ----. to fall, tumble, sink
16   **glōria, -ae** F. glory. Glōriā is ablative of reference.

2. FORTUNE PLANGO VULNERA

Fortūnē plangō vulnera
  stillantibus ocellīs,
quod sua michi mūnera
  subtrahit rebellis.
Vērum est, quod legitur,   5
  fronte capillāta,
sed plērumque sequitur
  Occāsiō calvāta.

In Fortūnē soliō
  sederam ēlātus,   10
prosperitātis variō
  flōre corōnātus;
quisquid tamen flōruī
  fēlix et beātus,
nunc ā summō corruī   15
  glōriā prīvātus.

The blows of Fortune I bewail
with overflowing eyes
for she withdraws from me her prize—
my efforts to no avail.
  Truer words were never writ:
  "Seize her by her forehead's hair;
  the back of her scalp is all bare!"

Once on her throne I was installed,
her garlands of glory on my brow;
relying on her loving vow
with visions of bliss I was enthralled.

VOCABULARY, *continued*

      privātus, -a, -um. deprived of (+ ablative case)
17 ***volvō**, 3, **volvī, volūtus.** to turn, rotate (intransitive in the passive voice)
18 **descendō**, 3, **descendī, descensum.** to fall, sink
      minorātus, -a, -um. diminished, less
20 **nimis** (adverb). too much, overmuch
      exaltō, 1. to exalt, raise
21 **vertex, verticis** M. top, peak, summit
22 **caveō**, 2, **cāvī, cautus.** to be on one's guard against, be aware of
      ruīna, -ae F. ruin, downfall
23 **axis, -is** M. axle of a wheel
24 **Hecuba, -ae** F. Hecuba, the wife of Priam, King of Troy
      rēgīna, -ae F. queen

2. FORTUNE PLANGO VULNERA, continued

Fortúnē rota volvitur:
   descendō minorātus;
alter in altum tollitur;
   nimis exaltātus   20
rēx sedet in vertice--
   caveat ruînam!
nam sub axe legimus
   Hecubam rēginam.

But as *she* sows, so do *I* reap—
   she knocked me down, that fickle dame,
snatched away my crown of fame!
   Beware of swift ruin!
On her wheel's axle clearly's seen
   the message: Hecuba WAS queen!

Hecuba Enslaved

This early woodcut depicting the delights which Venus awards her devotees is from a Swiss or German block-book printed around 1475. Note the bathers on the left--Californians evidently did not invent the "hot-tub"! (Illustrations from G. Whicher, *The Goliard Poets*; see Bibliography.)

Carmen 2 is a statement made by a particular poet of his experience in life with Fortuna. Orff has arranged it to be sung by the full chorus. What is the effect of a number of people making, in unison, such a personal statement?

Another epithet for Fortuna, *Occasio*, appears in *carmen* 2. *Occasio* is described as having hair only on the front of her head and being bald on the back of her head. Behind this odd description lies the idea that Fortune is fleeting; once she passes you by, you cannot "snatch" at her.

The poet states that the name of Hecuba is written on the axle of Fortuna's wheel. Hecuba was the wife of Priam, King of Troy, and mother of Hector. She is mentioned here because she had become an appropriate monitory example of Fortuna's capricious nature. Once the queen of a rich and proud city and mother of many fair daughters and valiant sons, after the fall of Troy, she became the slave of Ulysses, awarded to him by the drawing of lots. In Seneca's tragedy, *The Troades*, Hecuba sees that she has become an example of Fortuna's power and action in human life and mourns:

> Whoever trusts in his sovereignty, and
> lords it in his palace, not fearing
> the fickle gods, and thoughtlessly devotes
> his time to pleasure, let him look on me
> and you, O Troy. Never has Fortune given
> greater proofs on how fragile a position
> the proud stand.

> Quicumque regno fidit et magna potens
> dominatur aula nec leves metuit deos
> animumque rebus credulum laetis dedit,
> me videat et te, Troia. Non umquam tulit
> documenta fors maiora, quam fragili loco
> starent superbi.

We will be able to understand fully the significance of Hecuba as an emblematic figure of Fortuna's power only after we have read all the *carmina* in Orff's collection.

Finally, taking the two *carmina* together, what mood does Orff's musical arrangement create in you? As you listen to the *carmina* in the part "Primo Vere," see whether this mood is maintained in you by the *carmina* and by Orff's arrangement.

I
PRIMO VERE
UF DEM ANGER

CARMEN 3
CARMEN 4
CARMEN 5
CARMEN 6
CARMEN 7
CARMEN 8
CARMEN 9
CARMEN 10

This part of the *Carmina Burana* is divided into two sections, "Primo Vere" and "Uf dem Anger". As you glance over the *carmina* of Part I and listen to the selections, note what languages the *carmina* are written in. Despite their difference in this respect, Orff chose to unite these *carmina* into one part. As you read the *carmina* in the two sections, try to find a common theme or themes that unite the two sections. Do they give two contrasting pictures of what love and spring mean to two different groups of people?

VOCABULARY

1 *vēr, vēris N. spring

 *lēta (medieval Latin form): laetus, -a, -um. glad, happy

 *faciēs, -ēi F. face

2 propīnō, 1. to drink to a person by proposing a toast; to make a complementary present of; to give as a token of honor

3 hiemālis, -e. of winter, wintery

 aciēs, -ēi F. sharpness, bitterness

4 fugō, 1. to put to flight, drive away

5 vestītus, -ūs M. clothing, garment

6 Flōra, -ae F. Flora, goddess of flowers and spring

 prīncipor, 1. to reign, rule

7 nemus, nemoris N. woods, forest

 dulcisonus, -a, -um. sweet-sounding, pleasantly ringing

8 quē (medieval Latin form): quae

 cantus, -ūs M. song

 celebrō, 1. to celebrate, hymn, honor in song (here, of the song of birds)

9 Flōrē (medieval Latin form): Flōrae

 fundō, 3, fūdī, fūsus. to pour; stretch, extend

 gremium, -ī N. lap. Gremio = in gremio

10 Phēbus (medieval Latin form): Phoebus, -ī M. Phoebus the sun god

 novō mōre. Ablative of manner

11 rīsus, -ūs M. laugh, laughter

 hōc variō flōre. Ablative of means

12 stīpō, 1. to crowd, surround

13 Zephyrus, -ī M. Zephyrus, the gentle west wind associated with spring. Supply adest.

 nectareus, -a, -um. fragrant, sweet-smelling

14 spīrō 1. to breathe, blow

 odor, odōris M. odor, scent, smell

15 certātim (adverb). with rivalry, in competition

 bravium (medieval Latin form): brabeum, -ī N. prize, reward

16 currō, 3, cucurrī, cursus. to run, race, compete
 Currāmus is hortatory subjunctive, "Let us..."

 *amor, -ōris M. love

PRIMO VERE

3. VERIS LETA FACIES

Vēris lēta faciēs
  mundō propīnātur,
hiemālis aciēs
  victa iam fugātur,
in vestītū variō   5
  Flōra principātur,
nemorum dulcisonō
  quē cantū celebrātur.

Flōrē fūsus gremiō
  Phēbus novō mōre   10
rīsum dat, hōc variō
  iam stīpātur flōre.
Zephyrus nectareō
  spīrāns in odōre.
Certātim prō braviō   15
  currāmus in amōre.

Tipsy Spring with beaming smile lifts
  a toast
while defeated Winter limps off-field,
and the warm West Wind free
  once more
wafts the honeyed scent of flowers.

Birds lift their voices in praise as,
in dedaled robes Lady Flora awards
  the garland
to victorious Phoebus who rests in her
  embrace.
  (Let us, too, fight in the lists of love!)

VOCABULARY, continued

17 **cytharizō,** 1. to play the cithara (a Greek harp); to sing
canticum, -ī N. song
18 *****dulcis, -e.** sweet, pleasing
philomēna, -ae F. nightingale
19 **rideō,** 2, **rīsī, rīsum.** to smile, laugh
20 *****prātum, -ī** N. field
serēnus, -a, -um. clear, serene, bright, unclouded
21 **saliō,** 4, **saluī, saltum.** to leap, jump, hop
cētus (medieval Latin form): **coetus, -ūs** M. flock (of birds)
*****avis, -is** F. bird
22 **silvē** (medieval Latin form): **silvae**
amēna (medieval Latin form): **amoenus, -a, -um.** pleasant. Amēna is used here as a substantive.
23 **chorus, -ī** M. chorus
prōmō, 3, **prōmpsī, prōmptus.** to bring forth; utter
*****virgō, virginis** F. girl, maiden
24 *****gaudium, -ī** N. joy
millēnī, -ae, -a. thousands

3. VERIS LETA FACIES, continued

Cytharizat cantico
   dulcis philoména,
flóre rident varió
   práta iam seréna,   20
salit cétus avium
   silvé per aména,
chorus prómit virginum
   iam gaudia milléna.

The sweet nightingale pours forth her
   liquid note
under an unclouded sky; all meadows
   laugh with
waving flowers, while birds dance
   through
the greening forests.
   (Listen! I hear young girls a-Maying,
   singing of a thousand joys!)

Spring Plowing

The invention of the woodcut (see page 81) enabled artist to compose printed illustrations of great beauty and detail. This Renaissance example shows the goddess Flora with her gardening tools. Unlike medieval artists, Renaissance artists were allowed to show the female body nude or nearly so. (Illustration from *293 Renaissance Woodcuts for Artists and Illustrators,* a print of J. Amman's *Kunstbuchlin,* Dover Publishers, 1968.)

All the sensual delights--visual, aural, and olfactory--which spring provides us after the dulling chill of winter are praised and rejoiced over by the poet of *carmen* 3. He chooses, however, not to describe solely the rebirth of forest, flowers, and avian flocks, but also to emphasize the power of the life-force by personifying it through Flora, Phoebus, and even Zephyrus. Such mythological allegories for spring are common in medieval and Renaissance lyrics and art; one of the most famous and delicately beautiful paintings of spring's advent is Botticelli's "Primo Vere," which, like this *carmen,* is full of allegory and allusion. Is spring itself personified in lines 1-2? What is produced or begotten by the embrace of Flora and Phoebus in lines 11-12?

Winter in the medieval centuries was particularly a cold, stark time when life was lived totally inside the house. For a young man and woman in love there was little opportunity to meet except in the company of others. Consequently spring was particularly welcome, offering the young a chance to meet, flirt, and court in private or in groups of people their own age.

The most important festival celebrating spring was May Day. Its observance was a continuation of the pagan Roman festival *Floralia,* the festival of flowers. In medieval and Tudor England everyone arose at dawn to go "a-maying." Gathering budding branches and flowers, they hastened back into town to place them around a huge pole called the may-pole. A young girl was chosen to be "Queen of May," and, bedecked with flowers, presided over the dancing and festivities around the Maypole.

Perhaps the poet's mythological allegorization of spring might seem rather learned and formal at first; certainly it would seem so to the common folk dancing on the village green. Such a personification of nature brings into closer relationship the events in the world of nature and in the world of man. This close relationship explains the unexpected interjection of the poet and his audience in lines 15-16 into a poem which is essentially a description.

In the third stanza the poet mentions the nightingale, a bird renowned for its sweet singing and its association with spring and love. The mention of this bird, however, recalls yet another mythological character, Philomela, whose name is sometimes spelled Philomena. She was the sister to the queen of Thrace, Procne. Their fate is recounted by Ovid in the sixth book of his *Metamorphoses.* Tereus, king of Thrace, came to take Philomela on a visit to Procne, but fell in love with her. When they arrived in Thrace, he raped her, and fearing she would inform her sister, he cut out Philomela's tongue and abandoned her in a forest. To Procne he pretended that Philomela had died. Philomela, however, wove on a loom the story of her disgrace and sent the picture to Procne. Procne brought Philomela to the palace and determined to take vengeance on Tereus by killing their son, Itys. Cutting the body into pieces, she prepared a stew and served it to Tereus, and after he ate it, taunted him. Tereus, seizing his sword, pursued the two sisters, but the gods intervened, changing him into a hoopoe, Procne into a swallow, and Philomela into a nightingale.

VOCABULARY

1. **temperō,** 1. to regulate, rule
2. **pūrus, -a, -um.** pure
   subtīlis, -e. fine, nice, delicate
3. *****reserō,** 1. to unlock, unclose, open
4. **Aprīlis, -is** M. April, popularly thought to be derived from the verb aperiō, aperīre: quod vēr omnia aperit (Varrō, *Dē Linguā Latīnā* 6.33). Cf. reserat line 3.
5. *****properō,** 1. to hasten, rush
6. **herīlis, -e.** of man, man's
7. *****iocundus, -a, -um.** (of persons) pleasant, delightfully congenial (the type of person who makes a good lover--quī ad amōrem properat)
   imperō, 1. to give orders to, make demands on, exercise authority over (+ dative)
8. **puerīlis, -e.** childish, prankish
9. **rēs, rērum** F. pl. the things in the world, nature
   novitās, -ātis F. newness, renewal
10. **solemnis, -e.** formal, obedient to the laws of nature; solemn, ceremonial; festive
11. **auctōritās, -ātis** F. authority, force, influence, power
12. **gaudeō, 2, gavīsus** to rejoice
13. **viās = viās amōris**
    prēbet (medieval Latin form): **praebet**
    solitus, -a, -um. usual, accustomed, customary
14. **in tuō vēre** = in the springtime of your youth
15. **probitās, -ātis** F. correct behavior, honesty; sexual purity, virtue.
    In lines 15-16 supply tibi: "you have (enough) trust and virtue to keep your beloved."
16. **tuum = tuum amatōrem**
    retineō, 2, retinuī, retentus. to keep, retain.
    Retinēre is an infinitive substituting for a clause of result.

4. OMNIA SOL TEMPERAT

Omnia sōl temperat,
  pūrus et subtīlis,
novō mundō reserat
  faciem Aprīlis,
ad amōrem properat   5
  animus herīlis,
et iocundīs imperat
  deus puerīlis.

Rērum tanta novitās
  in solemnī vēre   10
et vēris auctōritās
  iubet nōs gaudēre;
viās prēbet solitās,
  et in tuō vēre
fides est et probitās   15
  tuum retinēre.

The royal Sun orders all things
  to put off Winter's veil, and
April uncovers her face to find
  a world renewed.
So men's hearts awaken to
  Love reborn
As the baby archer
  desires.

All nature is reborn,
  at Spring's command.
So we, too, must yield, rejoice
  to tread once more
Our former paths of love. Still —
  do not, my love,
Let your springing heart
  turn from my embrace!

VOCABULARY, *continued*

17 **fidēliter** (adverb). faithfully
18 **notō**, 1. to mark, note
21 **prēsentiāliter** (medieval Latin form): **praesentiāliter.** present
22 **absens.** participle used concessively: "although"
    remōtus, -a, -um. far off, removed.
    In remotā (viā) = on a distant journey
23 **quisquis, quidquid.** whoever, whatever
    tāliter (adverb). in such a way

4. OMNIA SOL TEMPERAT, continued

Amā mē fidēliter,
    fidem meam notā
dē corde tōtāliter
    et ex mente tōtā.   20
Sum prēsentiāliter
    absens in remōtā,
quisquis amat tāliter,
    volvitur in rotā.

Love me faithfully: mark my faithfulness
    in heart, in soul, in body.
Though I have gone far away,
    still — I hope —
My presence is not
    absent in your thoughts.
(Whoever loves in such a way
    is like one broke upon the wheel.)

You may have found this poem more difficult to translate into good English, even though the meanings of the individual words are clear. The poetical expression of *carmen* 4 is quite different from that of 3. In the latter, a picture was painted in words--and a picture is worth a thousand words. For example, which creates a more evocative picture of the sun shining warmly on spring's flowers: the statement, "the sun shines warmly" or the metaphor, "Phoebus laughs again, reclining on Flora's lap"? In *carmen* 4, statements rather than metaphors are used to describe the emotions spring awakens and you may paraphrase, if you wish, rather than translate literally, the poem to ensure clear transmission of the poet's thought from Latin to English.

Let us look more closely at individual words of *carmen* 4. As we do, review your translation of the *carmen* and, if necessary, revise your translation to make the poet's thought clearer in English.

The April sun is called *subtilis*. Why did the poet think this adjective particularly appropriate for the April sunshine as opposed, for example, to the sunshine of August? What is the popular etymology of "April"? Is this etymology recalled by the word *reserat?* The rhymes of lines 5-6 and 7-8 emphasize the contrast between *animus herilis properat* and *deus puerilis imperat.* Can you find an English rhyme that emphasizes the contrast? It may not be possible to translate all the poetical effects-- rhyme, metaphor, etc.--into another language! And finally who is the *deus puerilis?* Hint: he is generally depicted as a baby boy carrying bow and arrows.

Stanza 1 calls to mind Tennyson's line, "In the Spring a young man's fancy lightly turns to thoughts of love." Is the mood of stanza 2 as light-hearted as 1? Spring, called *leta* in *carmen* 3 and described as the bringer of a thousand joys, is called *solemnis* in line 10. In line 11, spring has *auctoritas* over us and orders *(iubet)*, not encourages, us to rejoice and love. The poet is here stating that we are subject to spring and hence to nature's laws. If the poet of this poem had once belonged to the church, this suggestion is not in accord with his former ecclesiastical principles. It would seem that lines 9-12 are key lines in this poem, the most explicit so far of Goliardic philosophy.

Carmen 4 celebrates the opportunity to love which spring gives young men, but our poet sees it also as giving him a reunion with his beloved. After the isolation imposed by winter, he is naturally worried about her faithfulness. His joy is dependent upon her *fides*. Thus he tells her in lines 14-16 *in tuo vere fides (tibi) est et probitas tuum (amorem) retinere,* and continues his exhortation in stanza 3. But stanza 3 concludes in a startling way--the poet ceases abruptly addressing his love when he utters the impersonal *quisquis*. He is stating for her (and for us all) an opinion he thinks is universally true. Are we to view this poem as a love-poem for the eyes of his beloved only, or is it intended for a wider audience as well?

The wheel, *rota,* with which the poem concludes, recalls the wheel of Fortune in *carmina* 1 and 2. But are we correct in identifying these two wheels with each other? In classical mythology there is another famous wheel, in Hades, the wheel of Ixion. Ixion tried to seduce Hera, queen of the gods and wife of Zeus. To punish him Zeus bound him to a whirling, fiery wheel. In medieval times, a common form of torture was to bind a person to a wheel which spun unceasingly. Is it the wheel of Fortune or the wheel of torture the poet has in mind? Can Fortune's wheel be viewed, in any way, as an instrument of torture? Is it ever possible for one to "jump off" it and cease being whirled around by Fortune?

VOCABULARY

1 **ecce** (interjection). Lo! Behold!
2 **optātus, -a, -um.** desired, wished for, longed for
3 **redūcō, 3, -duxi, -ductus.** to bring back, lead back
4 **purpurātus, -a, -um.** purple, rosy purple
6 **serēnō, 1.** to clear up, brighten, light up
7 **iamiam** (adverb). now

tristis, -e. sad, gloomy. Tristia is the adjective used as as a neuter substantive. Cēdant is hortatory subjunctive.

8 **ēstās** (medieval Latin form): **aestās, -ātis** F. summer
9 **recēdō, 3, -cessi, -cessum.** to go back, recede
10 **hyemis** (medieval Latin form): **hiems, hiemis** F. winter

sēvitia (medieval Latin form): **saevitia, -ae** F. severity, cruelty, harshness

11 **liquescō, 3, licui, ---.** to melt
13 **grandō, grandinis** F. hail

nix, nivis F. snow

cēterus, -a, -um. the rest, everything else

14 **brūma, -ae** F. winter
15 **sūgō, 3, sūxi, sūctus.** to suck
16 **ūber, ūberis** N. breast
17 **illī.** Dative of possession
19 *****lascīvō,·3, lascivi, lascītum.** to sport, frolic; be wanton
20 **dextera, -ae** F. right hand (grasped in greeting or as a token of agreement); pledge, contract; friendship

5. ECCE GRATUM

Ecce grātum
et optātum
vēr redūcit gaudia,
purpurātum
flōret prātum,   5
sōl serēnat omnia.
Iamiam cēdant tristia!
Ēstās redit,
nunc recēdit
hyemis sēvitia.   10

Iam liquescit
et dēcrescit
grandō, nix et cētera;
brūma fugit,
et iam sūgit,   15
vēr ēstātis ūbera;
illī mēns est misera,
quī nec vīvit,
nec lascīvit
sub ēstātis dexterā.   20

Ah!
welcome and long-desired
Spring
returns to us our former joys!
The gold-gleaming sun surges over
violet-spread fields
as Winter's dark chill ebbs.

Now
hail, snow, sleet and ice
vanish
while new-born Spring
nurses at Summer's breast.
He is a cold-hearted man
whose blood is
not heated at Summer's smile.

VOCABULARY, *continued*

21 *glōrior, 1. to boast, brag, vaunt. The subject of glōriantur et lētantur is defined by the relative clause (eī) quī cōnantur...ut (lines 24-26)

22 lētantur (medieval Latin form): **laetor**, 1. to rejoice, be glad

23 **mel, mellis** N. honey

   dulcēdō, -inis F. sweetness

24 cōnor, 1. to try; strive, contest

25 ūtor, 3, ūsus to use, enjoy; win (+ ablative)

26 prēmium (medieval Latin form): **praemium, -ī** N. reward, prize

   Cupīdō, -inis M. Cupid, the god of love

27 sīmus. Hortatory subjunctive

   iussus, -ūs M. order, command

   Cypris, Cypridis F. Venus, who was especially worshipped on the island of Cyprus.

30 esse. The basic construction of lines 27-30 is: sīmus...parēs esse Paridis ("May we, by Venus' command, boasting and rejoicing be equals of Paris").

5. ECCE GRATUM, continued

      Glōriantur
      et lētantur
in melle dulcēdinis,
      quī cōnantur
      ut ūtantur   25
prēmiō Cupīdinis;
sīmus iussū Cypridis
      glōriantēs
      et lētantēs
pārēs esse Paridis.   30

      Come!
    try your prowess at
      Love,
striving to gain Cupid's prize.
Venus commands us love-braggarts
    to rival Paris!

While medieval artists preferred to use their contemporaries or biblical figures in their illustrations, Renaissance artists responded to the revival of classical learning by turning to classical models and subjects. Phoebus Apollo is depicted here as the god in a pose similar to the Belvidere Torso of Apollonius. (Illustration from *293 Renaissance Woodcuts for Artists and Illustrators, op. cit.*)

Paris was a prince of Troy, one of King Priam's many sons. The illicit love between him and Helen, Queen of Sparta and Menelaus' wife, was the immediate cause of the Trojan War. Paris, by obeying the commands of Venus, became, for the Goliards, a model for lovers. The morality praised by this poem is not a morality approved of by the church which the Goliard had forsaken!

The poets of *carmina* 4 and 5 both make a statement about love and happiness which they believe applies to all men and women. Compare *carmen* 4, lines 23-24, with *carmen* 5, lines 17-20. In what way(s) are their attitudes towards love similar, in what way(s) dissimilar? The poet of *carmen* 5 urges us to love as our whims dictate *(lascivere)*, but the poet of *carmen* 4 urges his love to be faithful *(ama me fideliter)*. Perhaps we should think of the poet of *carmen* 5 as criticizing the poet of *carmen* 4 for taking a too serious, too restricting view of love.

The difference in attitude towards love and faithfulness of the two *carmina* is shown also in the difference between the two orchestrations Orff wrote. *Carmen* 3 opens with chimes. Several poems in the anthology of *Carmina Burana* are hymnlike, and these opening chimes prepare us for a serious hymn to spring, written in a solemn minor key. In medieval church services (and in certain churches today) chimes or bells were struck at important moments of the service, particularly during Holy Communion at the Invocation and Blessing of the Sacrament, to emphasize the presence of God. Does Orff's use of chimes suit the parody on a church hymn intended by the Goliardic poet? The solemnity of this *quasi*-hymn is enhanced by the *pianissimo* choral voices and delicate musical phrasing, which create a mood of awe appropriate for the presence of Flora, the goddess of spring.

Carmen 4, too, is a hymn-like song, opening with four bells and sung in a minor key. Lines 5-8 of each stanza are sung at a somewhat higher pitch than lines 1-4, but the segments have relatively little change in modulation, and the composition recalls the chants of church services.

The arrangement for *carmen* 5 is in a major key, expressive of the brightness and gaiety associated with spring. Orff has cleverly arranged this *carmen* like a tone-poem, in which the music aurally creates a visual picture of a frozen world becoming warm and alive. Line 1 of the first stanza begins with a chorus singing very softly in unison--the world is frozen. Then the tempo speeds up slightly and words are more choppily sung and resung, as the ice begins to melt and drops of water trickle from snow-laden branches and roofs. The chorus gradually increases in volume, singing lines 5-7 in a more flowing melody representing the flowing streams fed by the melting ice. Finally, voices in *fortissimo*, the chorus stresses each syllable of lines 8-10 in full force. This musical representation of the melting of snow and ice of winter is repeated as the chorus sings stanza 2, but the arrangement for stanza 3 is different, since spring has fully arrived. Instead, the exhortation of stanza 3 to love freely and boldly where one wills is sung loudly and boldly by the full chorus. Do you think Orff's orchestration for this *carmen* is effective?

Carmina 3, 4, and 5 link the advent of spring with the advent of love through mythological allusion and allegory. In language, imagery, and orchestration these *carmina* are significantly different from the *carmina* 6-10 in "Uf dem Anger." For which audience--the tavern or the home of a nobleman--are *carmina* 3, 4, and 5 suited?

UF DEM ANGER
(ON THE LAWN)

Except for *carmen* 6, the *carmina* in this section of Orff's work are selected from a distinct group of poems in the manuscript of Beuron (nos. 135-186). These poems usually have German stanzas as well as Latin ones. All are dance songs, and Orff begins this section of his work with *carmen* 6, a dance melody, to set the scene.

As it is today, dancing was a favorite activity in the medieval period, and clerics did not scorn to take part. In fact, frequently a priest would allow dancing inside his church during winter or inclement weather, despite prohibitions issued by the Pope. Songs such as these accompanied the dancing; the clerics sang the Latin verses, while women and girls sang the German ones.

While Orff includes elsewhere in his work songs from this section of the manuscript (*carmina* 17, 18, 19, 20, 22, 23), he selected the ones in "Uf dem Anger" for a special purpose. As you read the translations of the German verses and listen to the *carmina,* try to determine why Orff included this section in his work. What view of love does "Uf dem Anger" present? Do the folk *carmina* in "Uf dem Anger" use mythological references and allegory? Are the folk *carmina* as solemn as *carmen* 3 or are they more lighthearted?

VOCABULARY

2 *folium, -ī N. foliage
3 antīquus, -a, um. former
5 hinc (adverb). from here, away
   equitō, 1. to ride on horseback
6 *ēia (medieval Latin form): hēia (interjection). Oh!

Translation of German lines

8 so I long for my love.
9 The woods are all green:
10 why does my love stay so long away?
11 He has ridden away on horse-back.
12 Oh, Who now will love me?

UF DEM ANGER

6. Dance Without Words

7. Floret Silva

Flôret silva nôbilis
flôribus et foliis.
Ubi est antĭquus
meus amīcus?
Hinc equitâvit,
ēia, quis mē amābit?

Flôret silva undique,
nah mime gesellen is mir we.
Gruonet der walt allenthaben,
wa ist min geselle alse lange?
Der ist geriten hinnen,
o wi, wer sol mich minnen?

The forest's beauty spring
    retrieves
with glorious flowers, birds,
    and leaves.
Where is my lover of last year?
He's ridden far from here—
Alas, who will love me now?

The forest's ev'rywhere abloom
While I languish, dark in gloom.
Oh, why does he stay away?
He has ridden far away—
Alas, who will love me now?

VOCABULARY

Translation of German lines

    1 Shopkeeper, give me rouge
    2 to paint my cheeks
3-4 so that I will be irresistible to the young men.

    (Chorus)
    5 Look at me,
    6 young men!
    7 Don't I please you?

    8 Love one another, good men,
    9 kind women,
10-11 for love will make you noble and well-respected.

    (Chorus)
  12 Look at me,
  13 young men!
  14 Don't I please you?

15-16 O World, you are so rich in pleasures.
  17 I will always obey you,
  18 and through you be always loved.

    (Chorus)
  19 Look at me,
  20 young men!
  21 Don't I please you?

UF DEM ANGER

8. Chramer, gip die varwe mir

Chramer, gip die varwe mir,
 die min wengel roete,
 damit ich die jungen man
an ir dank der minnenliebe noete.

Shopkeeper! O Shopkeeper!
 Sell me some rouge,
 so I can make my cheeks
 all rosy-hued!
I must the young men attract,
all their minds and thoughts
  distract —
    to Love!

(Chorus)   Seht mich an,   5
                 jungen man!
                 lat mich iu gevallen!

O look, look, look at *me*,
 young men!
Don't you find me charming?

Minnet, tugentliche man,
 mennecliche frouwen!
 minne tuot iu hoch gemuot   10
unde lat iuch in hohen eren schouwen.

O love me, young men!
 O, I will love you!
 for Love is an honour,
 a prize won by few.
Do not my eyes, my lips attract,
all your minds and thoughts
  distract —
    to me?

(Chorus)   Seht mich an,
                 jungen man!
                 lat mich iu gevallen!

O look, look, look at *me*,
 young men!
Don't you find me charming?

Wol dir, werlt, daz du bist   15
 also freudenriche!
 ich will dir sin undertan
durch din liebe immer sicherliche.

O world, you are a trove
 of pleasure,
 of joy, of bliss, of delight
 beyond measure.
By your joys, your loves am I
  attracted,
my mind and thoughts by you
  distracted —
    to Love!

(Chorus)   Seht mich an,
                 jungen man!   20
                 lat mich iu gevallen!

O look, look, look at *me*,
 young men!
Don't you find me charming?

VOCABULARY

Translation of German lines

1 Here are the young girls
2 all in a circle;
3 they would like to be without men
4 all summer long!

5 Come, come, my sweetheart!
6 I am waiting for you,
7 I am waiting for you.
8 Come, come my sweetheart!

9 With your rosy, honeyed lips,
10 come and heal my heart!
11 Come and heal my heart,
12 with your rosy, honeyed lips!

13 Here are the young girls
14 all in a circle;
15 they would like to be without men
16 all summer long!

1 If I ruled all the world
2 from the sea to the Rhine,
3 I would give it all up
4 to hold the Queen of England
5 in my arms

UF DEM ANGER

9. Reie

Swaz hie gat umbe,
die sint alles megede,
die wellent an man
allen disen sumer gan!

Chume, chum, geselle min,   5
  ih enbite harte din,
  ih enbite harte din,
Chum, chum geselle min.

Suzen rosenvarwer munt.
  chum und mache mich gesunt,   10
  chum und mache mich gesunt,
suzer rosenvarwer munt.

Swaz hie gat umbe,
daz sint alles megede,
die wellent an man   15
allen disen sumer gan!

Here are we, maidens merry,
men's sweet words make us wary,
not for them will we tarry—
  all summer long!

Come, come, sweet-heart,
here I am, waiting for you,
  waiting for you,
yes, waiting for *you!*
Come, come my sweet sweet-heart!

With your rosy, honeyed, rosy lips,
come and heal my heart,
  heal my heart,
yes, heal *my* heart
with your rosy, honeyed, rosy lips!

Here are we, maidens merry,
men's sweet words make us wary,
not for them will we tarry—
  all summer long!

10 Were diu werlt alle min

Were diu werlt alle min
von deme mere unze an den Rin,
  des wolt ih mih darben,
daz diu chunegin von Engellant
  lege an minen armen!   5

Were the world all mine,
  to rule from the sea to the Rhine,
still I would yield it all
  to hold in loving thrall,
England's Queen!

The dress of these peasants shows they are from one of the countries in northern Europe. (Illustration from *293 Renaissance Woodcuts for Artists and Illustrators, op. cit.*)

48

The major keys of these dance-songs create a merry atmosphere ripe for joking, teasing, and flirting. *Carmen* 7 has a variety of special effects: a yodelling phrase, a short waltz, teasing dialogue between men and women, and a clever vocal effect of a man riding swiftly away. We should consider, however, whether Orff has selected at random *carmen* 7 as simply an example of another type of poetry the Goliards wrote for the common people. Both *carmen* 4 and *carmen* 7 concern lovers who have been separated. In both *carmina* the fidelity of their loved ones is at question. Can we regard these two *carmina* as expressing the attitude of the man (*carmen* 4) and the woman (*carmen* 7) in this love affair?

The quick, light notes of *carmen* 8 set the tone for the flirtatiousness of the words. This *carmen* originally came from a Passion play and was sung by Mary Magdalen, generally identified as the harlot who begged forgiveness from Jesus (*Luke* 7.36-8.3). Despite her request for cosmetics, the young woman seems quite confident of her beauty's power to attract many men. Is she as concerned with fidelity in love as the woman of *carmen* 7? Is the woman's attitude towards love in *carmen* 8 more similar to that of the man in *carmen* 4 or in *carmen* 5?

Another teasing dialogue between men and women is the arrangement for *carmen* 9, while the thought of *carmen* 10 is a satirical hyperbole reminiscent of the extravagant vows of Plautus' and Terence's love-struck youths. The English queen referred to may well have been Eleanor, Duchess of Aquitaine, about whom you will read more in the section, "Cour d'Amour." Can you imagine how the dancers would act out these songs on the lawn? This work of Orff's has been made into a film and has been staged for ballet; one of the more recent stagings is that of the *Grands Ballets Cannadiens*. If you were directing Orff's *Carmina Burana*, how would you stage this section of the work?

II
IN TABERNA

CARMEN 11
CARMEN 12
CARMEN 13
CARMEN 14

A greater contrast between the mood of this part of the *Carmina Burana* and that of "Uf dem Anger" is hard to imagine. Here we see the depths of despair to which the turn of Fortune's wheel can bring a man and how men react to the caprice of this fickle goddess.

The poet most admired by the other Goliards remains anonymous and is simply nicknamed by scholars as the "Archpoet." His best poem, outshining even any ecclesiastical hymn in rhyme and rhythm, is included in the *Carmina Burana* as *carmen* 11. Its meter proved so popular that it came to be used in contemporary hymnody and was called the "Goliardic."

VOCABULARY

*taberna, -ae F. tavern
1. estuans (medieval Latin form): aestuo, 1. to burn, to be on fire
   interius (adverb). inwardly, inside
2. ira, -ae F. anger, rage
3. amaritudo, -inis F. bitterness, despair
4. mee (medieval Latin form): meae
5. In lines 5-7, factus, cinis, and similis are a series of parallel nominatives.
6. cinis, cineris N. ashes
   elementum, -i N. element (here, the element of fire)
7. similis, -e. like to, similar to (+ dative)
8. de (preposition). with
   *ludo, 3, lusi, lusus. to play, frolic
9. cum (conjunction). although
   proprius, -a, -um. right, proper, fitting for (+ dative)
10. sapiens, sapientis. wise, sagacious, provident
11. petra, -ae F. rock, stone
12. sedes, -is F. a place to sit, a seat; resting place; site
    fundamentum, -i N. foundation (for a house or building)
13. stultus, -a, -um. foolish, stupid
    comparo, 1. to compare to, to liken to (+ dative)
14. fluvius, -i M. river
    labor, 3, lapsus to slip, glide, flow
15. sub (preposition). along
    trames, tramitis M. path, course
16. permaneo, 2, -mansi, -mansum. to remain, stay; last, continue

IN TABERNA

11. ESTUANS INTERIUS

Ēstuāns interius
  irā vehementī
in amāritūdine
loquor meē mentī:
factus dē materiā,   5
  cinis elementī,
  similis sum foliō,
  dē quō lūdunt ventī.

Cum sit enim proprium
  virō sapientī   10
suprā petram pōnere
  sēdem fundāmentī,
stultus ego comparor
  fluviō labentī,
sub eōdem trāmite   15
  nunquam permanentī.

Consumed with rage I yet compress
  my crescent anger;
in discontent beyond redress
  I decline soul's deliverance.
For I am not of spirit but of matter made
  — nay of *ash* of elementary fire! —
seared crisp like the crackling leaf
playtoy of the trifling wind.

The parable's prudent sage took heed
to shun the shaking, shifting sand
to set his house-foundation fast,
firm upon the stubborn stone.
But I — fool! fool! fool! — am like
spring's flashing flood,
always surging, always swirling,
its swollen stream along.

VOCABULARY, *continued*

17 **velutī** (adverb). just as, like
19 **āēr, āeris** N. air
20 *****vagus, -a, -um.** roaming, flitting
21 *****vinculum, -ī** N. chain, fetter, bond
22 **clāvis, -is** F. door-key
23 **quērō** (medieval Latin form): **quaerō, 3, quaesīvī, quaesītus.** to seek, search
24 **adiungō, 3, -iunxī, -iunctus.** to join with, associate with (+ dative)
    prāvus, -a, -um. depraved, vicious
25 **gravitās, -ātis** F. heaviness, seriousness
27 **iocus, -ī** M. joking, jesting
    amābilis, -e. likeable, lovable, pleasant
28 **fava, -ae** F. honey-comb
29 *****Venus, Veneris** F. Venus, the goddess of love
30 *****suāvis, -e.** pleasant, sweet, attractive
31 **quē** (medieval Latin form): **quae.** The antecedent is Venus.
32 **habitō, 1.** to live, dwell in
    ignāvus, -a, -um. lazy, sluggish; cowardly, faint-hearted
33 **gradior, 3, gressus** to go, wander, travel, rove
34 **mōs, mōris** M. custom, habit; manner. (ablative of manner)
    iuventus, -tūtis F. youth
35 **inplicō, 1.** to grasp, embrace, entwine
    vitium, -ī N. vice, corruption
36 **immemor, -oris.** unmindful, unheeding, disregarding (+ genitive)
37 **voluptās, ātis** F. pleasure, lust, debauchery
    avidus, -a, -um. greedy (+ genitive)
38 **salūs, salūtis** F. health; salvation
39 **mortuus, -a, -um.** dead
    anima, -ae F. soul, spirit
40 **gerō, 3, gessī, gestus.** to do. **cūram gerō,** to take care of (+ genitive)
    cutis, -is F. skin; flesh

11. ESTUANS INTERIUS, continued

Feror ego velutī
 sine nautā nāvis,
ut per viās āeris
 vaga fertur avis; 20
nōn mē tenent vincula,
 nōn mē tenet clāvis,
quērō mihi similēs
 et adiungor prāvīs.

Mihi cordis gravitās 25
 rēs vidētur gravis;
iocus est amābilis
 dulciorque favīs;
quicquid Venus imperat,
 labor est suāvis, 30
quē nunquam in cordibus
 habitat ignāvīs.

Viā lātā gradior
 mōre iuventūtis,
inplicor et vitiīs 35
 immemor virtūtis;
voluptātis avidus
 magis quam salūtis,
mortuus in animā
 cūram gerō cutis. 40

Unstably sails the skipperless ship,
 yawing, sprawling at wave's
  wild whim.
So do I. A small brown bird am I
 buffet-blown along
  the wind's wide ways.
Chains do not leash me,
 locks do not check me;
flitting everywhere I pursue
 the fraternity of the damned.

There lies the load of
 dull duty discarded;
as the busy bee sucks
 the blossom's bounty
I suck lively laughter's honey.
Whatever sweet Venus may command,
 I'm hers
her vassal, slave!
Her yoke is easy, her burden light —
faint-heart ne'er won that Fair Lady!

Sowing wild oats with wayward youths,
Hell's broad road I boldly rove;
vesting myself in Vice's lambent livery,
I leave lackluster Virture lay.
Sere Virtue's lures lure me not,
 when seductive Vice I seek —
salvation spurning, my soul unheeding,
I care only for my hide.

Modern dice are descendants of the carved knucklebones of animals which prehistoric man used in gambling. Dicing remained popular through the centuries, and in medieval times, people were so addicted to it that dicing schools (*scholae deciorum*) and guilds of dicers were established. In one game, possibly the one shown here, the object was to throw the three dice three times in an attempt to turn up three sixes. (Illustration from Benedictbeuern ms.)

    To judge from his poem, the Archpoet seems to have experienced the *vulnera fortune* (*carmen* 2). His misfortunes have taken from him all hope that Fortune's wheel will again raise him *in altum*. In his despair, to what consoling hope or ideal does he cling? Perhaps he has turned from Fortuna to Venus; if so, does he agree with the poet of *carmen* 8 that love ennobles a person? Does he agree with the words of *carmen* 5, *simus iussu Cypridis gloriantes et letantes pares esse Paridis*?

    Though he had earlier rejected service and a career in the church, with his life ordered by God's commandments, perhaps now the Archpoet believes his rejection was in error. Does he show any repentance in this *carmen*? The last line of *carmen* 11, *curam gero cutis*, is a parodying echo of a line which describes the Day of Judgment in the famous medieval hymn *Dies Irae*. On this day, Christians believe, Christ will return to the world to judge the living and the dead; the poet of the *Dies Irae* begs Christ *"Gere curam mei finis."* Such a parodying echo reveals that the Archpoet rejects entirely the church's beliefs about salvation, the soul's immortality, and life after death.

Read through *carmen* 11 again, and try to determine the Archpoet's attitude and emotions. In stanza 1, his emotion is obviously anger. Why might he be angry? At whom or at what is his anger directed? We might say he is "burning with anger," an expression so often used that the metaphor in it has ceased to be striking. What words or phrases, however, emphasize in a striking way the Archpoet's anger? Many medieval philosophers believed that the world was made out of four elements — air, earth, fire, and water — which combined in various ways to form animate and inanimate objects. A tree, for example, is made of the element earth, because it grows in the earth, of the element air, because it stretches into the air, and of fire, because it releases fire when burned. Of which element does the Archpoet say he is made? What is the effect of saying he is made of the ash (*cinis*) of the fire, rather than of fire itself? Though this idea of the physical nature of the world originated in the speculations of ancient Greek philosophers, many medieval theologians believed it true; consequently, in holding this belief, the Archpoet is not rejecting Christianity. But his proclamation, (*sum*) *factus de materia*, is not consonant with Christian belief for a Christian does not believe that he is composed of matter only. What does the Archpoet suggest when he compares himself to a leaf blown hither and thither by the winds?

Stanza 2 also has veiled references to Christian beliefs and ideals that the Archpoet still rejects. Lines 9-11 refer to a parable told by Jesus (*Matt.* 7.24-27 and *Luke* 6.46-49). In this parable, a wise man builds his house upon a rock, and a foolish man his upon the sand. During a terrible storm the house built on sand collapses because of its unstable foundation, but the house of the wise man stands securely. Also within these lines of stanza 2 is a reference to another event related in the Gospel of St. Matthew. In the twelfth century, all orthodox Christians of Western Europe considered the Pope in Rome the spiritual head of the church on earth. The Pope's claim to such ultimate authority derives from his being the direct successor, as Bishop of Rome, of St. Peter. St. Peter's primacy among the other bishops is established, as Catholic theologians argue, from Christ's words to Simon, "Thou art Peter, and upon this rock I will build my church . . ." (*Matt.* 16.13-19. "Peter" in Greek means "rock.") The Archpoet admits he is the *stultus*, the foolish man in the parable in not building his life on a firm foundation, that is, on the Pope and the Church. If he realizes his stupidity, why, do you suppose, does he prefer to be like an unstable, gliding river?

57

The last stanza refers implicitly to an important Christian belief that a person is only really and truly alive if he believes in Christ. If the Archpoet is *mortuus in anima* as a Christian, what does he have in his heart instead of Christ?

Carmen 11, it is clear, deserves its high repute as the best Goliardic poem, not just for its exemplary rhythm and rhyme, but for the skill with which the poet expresses his thoughts subtly by parody, indirect reference, and metaphor.

Orff's arrangement is a musical interpretation of the poem. As you listen to it, consider how the arrangement expresses the mood of the poet. What mood does the music create in you? What is the relationship of the rhythm to the words? Take note of the raging gallop to which are set the lines *estuans interius ira vehementi*, the jerky rhythm for *feror ego veluti sine nauta navis, ut per vias aeris vaga fertur avis*. Orff expresses the bravado of *non me tenent vincula, non me tenet clavis* by the broad notes of this musical phrase.

Carmina 12, 13, and 14 are such as the *pravi amici* of the Archpoet were wont to sing. Their mood is one of jesting mingled with bitterness, of boasting covering a fearful despair. As you translate these *carmina*, consider what musical arrangement would suit each. Do Orff's arrangements surprise you? Do they suit the *carmina*?

VOCABULARY

    cignus, ī M. swan
    ūrō, 3, ussī, ustus. to burn, roast
    cantō, 1. to sing
1   **ōlim** (adverb). once, formerly
    lacus, -ūs M. lake
    colō, 3, coluī, cultus. to live in, dwell in, inhabit
2   ***pulcher, -chra, -chrum.** beautiful, lovely, handsome
    extō, 1, exstitī, ---. to stand forth, be prominent or conspicuous
5   ***niger, -gra, -grum.** black
6   **fortiter** (adverb). very much, strongly
7   **gīrō, 1.** to turn on a spit
    regīrō, 1. to turn again and again on a spit
    garcifer, -ī M. boy, servant
8   **rogus, -ī** M. fire
9   **propīnō 1.** to serve, set down on a table
13 **scutella, -ae** F. salver, serving dish
    iaceō, 2, iacuī, iacitum. to lie, rest
14 **volitō, 1.** to fly
    nequeō, 4, -īvī, -ītum. to be unable
15 **dēns, dentis** M. tooth
    frendō, 3, -uī, ---. to gnash, grind

IN TABERNA

12 OLIM LACUS COLUERAM

Cignus ustus cantat:
Olim lacūs colueram,
ōlim pulcher extiteram,
dum cignus ego fueram.
   Miser, miser!
   modo niger   5
et ustus fortiter!

Girat, regirat garcifer;
mē rogus urit fortiter;
propīnat mē nunc dapifer.
   Miser, miser!   10
   modo niger
et ustus fortiter!

Nunc in scutellā iaceō,
et volitāre nequeō,
dentēs frendentēs videō!   15
   Miser, miser!
   modo niger
et ustus fortiter!

Once on placid lake I floated
once I of great beauty boasted —
a snow-white swan!
   Oh, woe, woe, woe,
   to the table I go!

Now with *fines herbes* am I coated,
by the fire soundly roasted —
"guest of honour" anon!
   Oh, woe, woe, woe,
   to the table I go!

Look! Served up on a platter,
my bones the diners scatter —
their teeth gnash, mash, gash!
   Oh, woe, woe, woe,
   to the table I go!

This is quite literally a "swan song"! The origin of this expression lies in the belief that when a swan came to the end of its life, it swam out into the middle of its lake and sang one last, most sweet song before sinking beneath the waters. What sort of melody and key do you expect Orff will use in his arrangement? By now doubtless you will guess he will not use the obvious, especially since we have here a setting quite different from a placid lake — a dining room full of hearty eaters waiting for the specialty of the house!

We should not consider this poem as simply a "sick" joke. After the emotional climax Orff has produced in *carmen* 11, such a "joke" would seem out of place. Besides you have realized by now that a Goliardic poem should never be read solely on the "surface" level. We must look at *carmen* 12 from the aspect of the spiritual philosophy which is the core of *carmen* 11.

The two *carmina* concern the same theme — physical and spiritual mortality. Let us see whether they are similar to any extent in imagery. The poet of *carmen* 12 sings in the guise of a swan. To what animal does the poet of *carmen* 11 liken himself? In the final lines of *carmen* 11, the Archpoet proclaims he takes "care of his skin" first of all. What is happening to the flesh of the swan in carmen 12? We noted that the final lines of *carmen* 11 were a parody of the hymn *Dies Irae* which describe the Day of the Last Judgment when sinful souls will be sent to Hell to burn forever. Can the fire roasting the swan be a metaphor for the fire of Hell? If so, the swan's cry "*Miser, miser modo niger et ustus fortiter*" is a particularly poignant way of describing the sinful poet's ultimate fate. Medieval illustrations of Hell often show its entrance as the sharp-toothed jaws of a monster gaping wide; do you suppose this image of Hell lies behind the words of this *carmen*? If so, who, then, really are the diners? The poem has one clever sound effect: what motion does your mouth make in saying the words *dentes frendentes*?

Orff has composed a very eerie song, begun by a wailing clarinet solo. How does the tenor singer emphasize this eeriness? The swan/poet sings slowly, sadly, but the chorus sings in a quick rhythm, reaching a crescendo on each last line of the refrain. What do these two different orchestrations reveal about the mood of the swan/poet and diners/devils?

VOCABULARY

1. **abbas, abbatis** M. abbot

   Cucaniensis, -is F Cockaigne or Cucany, an imaginary land of idleness and plenty sung about by the Goliards. Its name comes from the Old French pais de cocaigne, "land of cakes." In this country, houses were built of cake, roast geese wandered through the streets, larks fell already cooked and buttered from the sky, and rivers and fountains ran with wine. Cucany remained in the poetic imagination down through the seventeenth century and influenced the development of the American myth of "The Big Rock Candy Mountain" of the hoboes.

2. **consilium, -ī** N. deliberation, counsel; council, senate; church council

   bibulus, -ī M. a drinker

3. **secta, -ae** F. sect, group

   Decius, -ī M. Publius Decius Subulo, a supporter of the Gracchi and tribune in 120 B.C., was infamous for his dissolute conduct. Accused of extortion in 119 B.C., he was acquitted, doubtless due to the efforts of the equites who supported him against the optimates. He died soon after 115 B.C.

   voluntās. -ātis F. wish, inclination

4. **manē** (adverb). in the morning

   quēsierit (medieval Latin form): **quaesiverit.**

5. **vespera, -ae** F. evening

6. **dēnūdō,** 1. to strip bare, strip naked

   vestis, -is F. clothing (ablative of separation)

7. **Wafna** (German exclamation). To arms! To arms!

8. **turpis, -e.** ugly, foul; base

9. **nostrē vitē** (medieval Latin form): **nostrae vitae**

10. **auferō, auferre, abstulī, ablātus.** to take away, steal

IN TABERNA

13 EGO SUM ABBAS

Ego sum abbas Cucaniensis
et consilium meum est
 cum bibulīs,
et in sectā Deciī voluntās
 mea est,
et quī manē mē quēsīerit
 in tabernā,
post vesperam nūdus
 ēgrediētur,   5
et sīc dēnūdātus veste
 clāmābit:

Wafna, wafna!
 quid fēcistī sors
 turpissima?
Nostrē vitē gaudia
 abstulistī omnia!   10

I am the Abbot
of Big Rock Candy Mountain
and I baptize my monks with pure
 gin!
Drunk I have lived, drunk may I die!
Down to Hell may my soul fly!

He who asks me to shrive his soul,
will leave my presence purse wholely
 empty, weeping and moaning:

"Wafna! Wafna!
 What have you done, foul
 Fortune?
You have taken away all my joy
 in life!"

65

One of the tortures of Hell was the roasting or stewing of the damned souls. Scenes such as this were placed not only in devotional books, but were also carved on the facades of cathedrals or painted on church walls as a warning to the unrepentant sinners. (Fifteenth century German woodcut, British Museum.)

A solo baritone sings this *carmen* as a mock church chant: here our Goliard plays "abbot" before a rowdy tavern group of drunkards — a more incongruous meeting of the worlds of church and Goliard can hardly be imagined. The Goliard reveals himself as an inveterate gambler, and rather than freeing a person of his sins, the Goliard "frees" him of his garments and money.

The theme of *sors* or *Fortuna* reappears in this *carmen*. The Goliard, profitting by his opponent's bad luck, *in altum tollitur* (*carmen* 2). But he should beware of ruin! *Caveat ruinam! Sors* is *turpissima* and *variabilis* — it can take away all the joys of his life, too.

This *carmen* is also connected in theme and thought to *carmina* 11 and 12 since this Goliard is *voluptatis avidus magis quam salutis.* Is he therefore *mortuus in anima* as well?

VOCABULARY

1 **quandō** (conjunction). when
2 **cūrō,** 1. to care for, take heed of, be mindful of
   humus, -ī F. earth; grave; death
3 **lūdus, -ī** M. gambling game, dicing
4 **insūdō,** 1. to sweat (+ dative)
5 The prose order of lines 5-8 is: (sī cuīquam) hōc est opus ut quaerātur quid agātur in tabernā ubi nummus est pincerna, audiātur sīquid loquar.
6 **nummus, -ī** M. money
   pincerna, -ae M. cup-bearer, butler; bringer of food and drinks
7 **opus est.** there is need, it is necessary (impersonal verb followed by an ut-clause
   quērātur (medieval Latin form): **quaerātur**
8 **sī quid.** Equivalent to **sī aliquid,** "if...anything"
9 **quīdam, quaedam, quoddam.** some
   lūdō, 3, **lūsī, lūsus.** to gamble, play a game of chance
   bibō, 3, **bibī, bibitus.** to drink
10 **indiscrētē** (adverb). indiscreetly, shamelessly
11 The prose order of lines 11-14 is: sed ex hīs quī in lūdō morantur, quīdam dēnūdantur, etc.
13 **vestiō,** 4, **-īvī, -ītus.** to clothe, dress
14 **saccus, -ī** M. sackcloth, rags
   induō, 3, **induī, indūtus.** to dress, to clothe
16 **Bacchus, -ī** M. Bacchus, the god of wine; by metonymy, wine itself
   mittō, 3, **mīsī, missus.** to send; throw, cast
   sors, sortis F. dice
17 **nummāta, -ae** F. a pennyworth. The sense of line 17 is: sortēs prō nummāta vīnī mittuntur, i.e., in order to determine who will pay for the drinks.

IN TABERNA

14 QUANDO SUMUS

In tabernā quandō sumus,
nōn cūrāmus quid sit humus,
sed ad lūdum properāmus,
cui semper insūdāmus.
Quid agātur in tabernā,   5
ubi nummus est pincerna,
hōc est opus ut quērātur,
si quid loquar, audiātur.

Quīdam lūdunt,
   quīdam bibunt,
quīdam indiscrētē vīvunt.   10
Sed in lūdō quī morantur,
ex hīs quīdam dēnūdantur,
quīdam ibi vestiuntur,
quīdam saccīs induuntur.
Ibi nullus timet mortem,   15
sed prō Bacchō mittunt
   sortem:

When we're drinking at the bar
the least of all our worries are
our death and fate beyond the grave.
We'd rather sweat o'er the roulet table
for as long as we are able —
our money and credit we hope to save!
What's going on in here
where a buck will get you beer?

Some men gamble, some get boozy,
others flirt with a floozy,
but of those who stay with dice,
some loose money, pants, and shirt
while others (a few) hit pay dirt.
All are lost in forms of vice;
while they can raise a glass
they care not for what may
   come to pass.

VOCABULARY, *continued*

18 **libertīnus, -ī** M. libertine, wastrel
19 **semel** (adverb). once; here apparently it means "once again."
20 **hēc** (medieval Latin form): **haec**
   ter (adverb). thrice
21 **quater** (adverb). four times
   Christiānus, -ī M. a Christian
   cunctus, -a, -um. all
22 **quinquiēs** (adverb). five times
   fidēlis, -e. faithful; believing, i.e. Christian
   dēfunctus, -a, -um. dead, deceased
23 **sexiēs** (adverb). six times
   soror, sorōris F. lay sister, a woman associated with a religious order, but who has not taken her final vows as a nun.
24 **septiēs** (adverb). seven times
   silvānus, -a, -um. of the woods of forest. Mīlitēs silvānī were outlaws, like Robin Hood.
25 **octiēs** (adverb). eight times
   frāter, frātris M. friar
   perversus, -a, -um. sinning, erring
26 **noniēs** (adverb). nine times
   monachus, -ī M. monk
27 **deciēs** (adverb). ten times
28 **undeciēs** (adverb). eleven times
   discordō, 1. to be at odds with someone, angry at someone
29 **duodeciēs** (adverb). twelve times
   pēnitentibus (medieval Latin form): **paenitentibus. paeniteō, 2, -uī, ---.** to be penitent, repentant, sorrowful
30 **trediciēs** (adverb). thirteen times
   agō, 3, ēgī, actus. to do; **iter agere,** to journey, travel
31 **tam...quam.** both...and, alike
   pāpa, pāpae M. the Pope
32 **lex, lēgis** F. law; limit; moderation

14. QUANDO SUMUS, continued

Prīmō prō nummāta vīnī,
ex hāc bibunt lībertīnī;
semel bibunt prō captīvīs,
post hēc bibunt ter prō vīvīs   20
quater prō Chrīstiānīs
    cūnctīs,
quīnquiēs prō fidēlibus
    dēfūnctiīs,
sexiēs prō sorōribus vānīs,
septiēs prō mīlitibus silvānīs.

Octiēs prō frātribus perversīs,   25
noniēs prō monachīs dispersīs,
deciēs prō nāvigantibus,
undeciēs prō discordantibus,
duodeciēs prō pēnitentibus,
tredeciēs prō iter agentibus.   30
Tam prō pāpā quam prō rēge
bibunt omnēs sine lēge.

First the dice decide who pays —
his generosity we all do praise!
Secondly we toast all in jail,
then all those who are hearty and hale.
Fourth we toast all Christians good,
then the faithful departed brotherhood!
Sixth we toast all false nuns,
then all robbers bearing guns!

Eighth for friars full of sin,
ninth for those in monasteries
    no longer "in"!
Tenth for those on broad sea sailing,
eleventh for wives nagging and railing.
Twelfth for all those who sins recant,
thirteenth for parolee "emigrant"!
Drink to the Pope! Drink to the King!
Drink to them — to anything!

VOCABULARY, continued

33 **hera, -ae** F. mistress of a house
   herus, -i M. master of a house
34 **clerus, -i** M. clerk; minister, clergyman
36 **servus, -i** M. servant
   ancilla, -ae F. maidservant
37 **velox, velocis.** energetic, swift
   piger, pigra, pigrum. lazy, slothful, shiftless
38 **albus, -a, -um.** white
39 **constans, constantis.** settled, stay-at-home
40 **rudis, -e.** rough, illiterate
   magus, -i M. wise man, scholar
41 **pauper, paupera, pauperum.** poor, penniless
   egrotus (medieval Latin form): **aegrotus, -a, -um.** sick, ill
42 **exul, exulis** M. an exile, banished person
   ignotus, -a, -um. unknown, strange
43 **canus, -a, -um.** old, white-haired
44 **presul** (medieval Latin form): **praesul, praesulis** M. bishop
   decanus, -i M. deacon
46 **anus, -us** F. old woman

14. QUANDO SUMUS, *continued*

Bibit hera, bibit herus,
bibit miles, bibit clerus,
bibit ille, bibit illa   35
bibit servus cum ancilla.
Bibit velox, bibit piger,
bibit albus, bibit niger,
bibit constans, bibit vagus,
bibit rudus, bibit magus.   40

Bibit pauper et egrotus,
bibit exul et ignotus,
bibit puer, bibit canus,
bibit presul et decanus,
bibit soror, bibit frater,   45
bibit anus, bibit mater,
bibit ista, bibit ille,
bibunt centum, bibunt mille.

The wife drinks, the husband drinks,
the soldier drinks, the priest drinks,
he drinks, she drinks,
barkeeper drinks, waitress drinks,
workingman drinks, bum drinks,
everyone drinks!
The stay-at-home drinks,
    the traveller drinks,
the ignorant and the learned drink!

The poor man drinks and
    the sick man drinks,
the exile and the immigrant drink,
the Bishop and the Elder!
Sister drinks, brother drinks,
grandma drinks, mommy drinks,
she drinks, he drinks,
one hundred drink, one thousand!

VOCABULARY, *continued*

49 **parum** (adverb). hardly, scarcely
   sexcentē (medieval Latin form): **sexcentae. sexcentī, -ae, -a.**
   six hundred, a proverbially infinite number
   nummātē (medieval Latin form): **nummātae. nummāta, -ae** F. coin
50 **dūro**, 1. to last, last out, suffice
   immoderātē (adverb). freely, immoderately
51 **mēta, -ae** F. limit, end
52 **quamvīs** (conjunction). although (+ subjunctive)
   lētā (medieval Latin form): **laetus, -a, -um**
53 **rōdō, 3, rōsī, rōsus.** to gnaw; backbite, complain; slander
   gens, gentis F. tribe; a group of people
54 **egens, egentis.** poor, needy
55 **confundō, 3, -fūdī, -fūsus.** to confound, throw into disorder.
   quī...confundantur...scrībantur. subjunctives expressing wishes
56 **scrībō, 3, scrīpsī, scrīptus.** to write; enroll, list

74

14. QUANDO SUMUS, *continued*

Parum sexcentē nummatē
dūrant, cum immoderātē 50
bibunt omnēs sine mētā.
Quamvīs bibant mente lētā,
sīc nōs rōdunt omnēs gentēs
et sīc erimus egentēs.
Quī nōs rōdunt confundantur 55
et cum iustīs nōn scribantur.

Fort Knox doesn't have enough gold
to pay for all the beer we can hold!
When we drink, there is good cheer,
but there are those who carp and jeer
that we to Hell are going fast —
well, we will have the best laugh at last,
they'll have *each other's* company
   in Heaven!

The last of these mocking, defiant tavern songs essentially states that the whole world engages in aimless pleasures represented by ceaseless drinking. As you listen to the *carmen*, note the changes in rhythm and tone and the way the music expresses the insanity of this aimless drinking and the defiance of the Goliards who are *voluptatis avidi* and care only for their *cutis* and not for their *animae*.

Carmen 14, like *carmina* 11, 12, and 13, expresses the theme of the Goliardic devotion to earthly pleasures and the rejection of spiritual values. This *carmen*, too, must be read on two levels — the surface level, on which it is a funny drinking song, and on a subsurface level, on which it is a bitter and scornful statement of Goliardic philosophy. Its themes of drinking, pleasure, and gambling link it to *carmen* 13, in which the gambling losses are not solely material losses, but are metaphors for the loss of spiritual values. As in *carmen* 13, clerical and secular lives mingle, for *carmen* 14 can be seen as a parody of the Mass. During the Mass, the congregation and priest pray for "the whole state of Christ's church," mentioning those engaged in various occupations as well as their own friends and family. Instead of praying for the souls of priests, nuns, the dead, the living, etc., what do the Goliards do? Note that the pope and king are recipients of their unceasing toasts (rather than unceasing prayers)!

The broad survey of humanity whom the Goliard toasts in lines 17-32 is seen also in lines 33-48, in which all humanity joins in unending drinking. How does the music represent aurally this frenzied activity? In lines 52-56, the Goliard again protests life is unfair to him and treats him cruelly. Other people slander him and his fellows, but in turn the Goliards scoff others' opinions. Lines 55-56 refer again to the *Dies Irae*, the day of Final Judgment. St. John, in exile on the isle of Patmos, wrote the *Book of Revelation* after he had a vision of the last days of the world and the Day of Judgment. On that day, he said, Christ will enter the names of the just in "The Book of Life" (*Rev.* 3.5). But who, in the opinion of the Goliards, are the *iusti*?

Before beginning the third section of the *Carmina Burana*, we need to review the sections we have read and heard to re-examine the connection(s) between them. Certainly more disparate views on life and love could not be made. The initial Fortuna section is linked in tone to the "In Taberna" section: the uncertainty of life and fortune can breed in a man cynicism, selfishness, and despair. The mood of the "In Taberna" section is in direct contrast to the mood of the lovers, scholar and peasant alike, in the section "Primo Vere." In that section, spring, the loveliest time of the year, is described as if it were Paradise itself. Even rude peasants feel the power of Love, which is so strong that it enriches all (*carmen* 8). To live and be in love is to live a *beata vita*. To be separated from one's lover is torture (*carmen* 4, line 24).

Another dimension to this delightful picture of life, love, and spring is revealed in the *carmina* of the section "In Taberna." The Archpoet devotes himself to Venus and love. Though he agrees that love brings him delight and pleasure (*quicquid Venus imperat labor est suavis*), he does not experience love as an ennobling passion. He describes himself as *mortuus in anima*, dead in spirit. He is alive only in his body which is fragile and perishable (*carmen* 11, lines 5-8). The Archpoet does realize that by discarding the Church, and its promise of a *beata vita* in Paradise, he has sentenced himself to the material world and its material pleasures which, like his body, will perish and decay. Looking at his life, devoted to Venus and love, would you say that it is a *beata vita*?

Part III, the "Court of Love," hearkens back to Part I, for it pictures love as a union of spirit and body that is not restricted to a particular social group; *carmen* 16 and 18 are sung with Latin verses alternating with verses written in Old French and Old German and are thus somewhat akin in form to those in the subsection "Uf dem Anger."

III
COUR D'AMOUR
THE COURT OF LOVE

CARMEN 15
CARMEN 16
CARMEN 17
CARMEN 18
CARMEN 19
CARMEN 20
CARMEN 21
CARMEN 22
CARMEN 23
CARMEN 24

Andreas asked, "Between what persons may love exist?" The Countess of Champaigne conferred with her ladies and replied, "Love properly exists between two persons who, being of equal social rank, could marry but are not married." Andreas pursued his point, "What status has a cleric as a lover?" The Countess Marie declared, "His status as a lover depends upon the rank and standing of his parents."

These decisions given by Marie, the Countess of Champaigne, in consultation with her ladies and her mother, Queen Eleanor of Aquitaine and wife of Henry II, King of England, were written down by Andreas Capellanus in his book, *De Arte Honeste Amandi* (On the Art of Loving Properly), in the early thirteenth century. (His title hints that he had in mind an earlier book which guided would-be lovers in their affairs of the heart, the *Ars Amatoria*, or *Art of Love* written by the poet Ovid.) Andreas Capellanus (fl. 1175-1180), chaplain to Marie, Countess of Champaigne, defined in his book what is meant by courtly or romantic love.

The concept of "courtly love" appeared quite suddenly in the area of southern France, called Languedoc, at the end of the eleventh century. Courtly love conceived of love as a shining, ideal relationship between man and woman, although this ideal relationship was hardly a moral one in the eyes of the Church. The lover guided his actions by a refined notion of humility and courtesy: he was his lady's vassal and without demur, almost abjectly perhaps, submitted to her slightest request. As a reward he hoped to be accepted as her lover, but he did not hope to marry her -- in fact she was probably married already. Love, in the courtly sense, was thought as an emotion foreign to marriage and quite different from the marital affection which should exist between husband and wife. Affection owed one's spouse is not affection granted freely, and love was an emotion to be granted of one's own free will. A noble emotion, transfiguring lover and beloved -- so it was conceived by the poets of Languedoc who created essentially a religion of love.

The notion of romantic love created by the Languedoc troubadours apparently is an original idea, for love in this sense is unknown to the lyric poets of Rome, Catullus and Ovid. Yet the latter in some way served the troubadours as a source of inspiration, for Ovid, in his *Ars Amatoria*, makes Amor, or Cupid, his supreme god and love a religion --though he does all this in a very facetious manner. Certainly the Goliards also made love into a mock religion, but they mocked Christianity, not Jupiter. The bishop prayed to the Virgin Mary, Queen of Heaven; the Goliard prayed to Venus, adapting the bishop's prayer for his own purpose: he has "sinned" against her in not loving and asks for "absolution" so that he may live in a "state of grace."

The *carmina* in the section "Cour d'Amour" are arranged in the form of a dialogue between the poet and his lady love with a "court", the chorus, commenting on the scene. Orff's arrangement is modelled upon the "Court of Love" of the Countess Marie which discussed the conduct of lovers and gave those decisions contained in Andreas' *De Arte Honeste Amandi*.

Since the love Cupid inspired in the courtly love ethic was extra-marital and unholy, the cherubic baby god has been metamorphosed into a bat-winged devil actively encouraging the young lovers. This illustration is an example of the woodcut form of illustration; the artist carved the block of wood to leave the lines forming the illustration. The carved block was inked and then pressed on paper. The woodcut originated in northern Europe in the middle of the 1400's and was a development springing from the movable print invented by Gutenberg. (Illustration from *Der Seelentrost*, Augusburg, 1478; taken from G. Whicher, *The Goliard Poets;* see Bibliography.)

VOCABULARY

1. **volō,** 1. to fly
2. **libīdō, libīdinis** F. desire
3. *****iuvenis, -is** M. youth, young man
   iuvenculē (medieval Latin form): **iuvenculae. iuvencula, -ae** F. young girl, maiden
4. **coniungō, 3, -iunxī, -iunctus.** to join together, unite
   meritō (adverb). rightly, deservedly
5. *****sīquis, sīqua, sīquid.** if any man, woman, thing
   socius, -ī M. lover
   The thought of lines 5-6 is: sīqua puella sine sociō est, caret omnī gaudiō.
6. **careō, 2, caruī, ---.** to lack, miss (+ ablative)
   gaudium, -ī N. joy, pleasure, delight
7. **infimus, -a, -um.** lowest, deepest, darkest. Paraphrase "noctis infima" ("the lowest things of the night") as "despair" (at not having a lover).
8. **intimus, -ī** M. the inmost part
9. **custōdia, ae** F. a place for safe-keeping; custody
10. **rēs, reī** F. thing; situation, plight; fate
    amārus, -a, -um. bitter, sorrowful

COUR D'AMOUR

15. AMOR VOLAT UNDIQUE

Amor volat undique,	The God of Love flies everywhere
captus est libīdine.	casting wide his net of desire.
Iuvenēs, iuvenculē	Young men, young girls,
coniunguntur meritō.	are rightly caught together.
Sīqua sine sociō, 5	If a girl has no lover,
caret omnī gaudiō;	she lacks all happiness;
tenet noctis infima	her heart's gloom is
sub intimō	midnight thick —
cordis in custōdiā:	*her* fate is bitterest of all!
fit rēs amārissima. 10	

Study of classical statues gave Renaissance artists a better understanding of human anatomy. Whereas medieval artists tended to present the human figure frontally, with elongated limbs (see page 88 for an example), the Renaissance artists knew the proportions of the human body, at its different ages, and were intrigued with the problems different positions of the body presented them. Here a baby's body is shown in a position requiring the artist to foreshorten the limbs and lower body. (Illustration from *293 Renaissance Woodcuts for Artists and Illustrators, op. cit.*)

Though *carmen* 15 is a poem of ten short lines, it plays an important thematic role in the *Carmina Burana,* serving as an introduction to the section "Cour d'Amour," and also as a link to the *carmina* of the earlier sections. What idea(s) in *carmen* 4 do the words *amor volat undique* recall to mind? What thought(s) in *carmen* 5 do the words *iuvenes, iuvencule, coniunguntur merito* echo?

So short a poem to serve as such a summary! As did *carmen* 1, this poem suggests many things in a few words -- *multum in parvo!* Particularly elliptical in thought are the words *tenet noctis infima sub intimo cordis in custodia,* through which the poet analyzes the loverless girl's emotions. Is she hopeful of new love or despairing of happiness? Does she express this emotion outwardly or does she keep it to herself? In translating this complexity of thought and emotion, you may have to paraphrase to make clear the poet's words.

VOCABULARY

2 **michi** (medieval Latin form): **mihi**
3 **colloquium, -i** N. voice, conversation

Translation of French lines
4 make me weep,
5 and make me sigh,
6 and make me more fearful.

7 **sodālis, -is** M. friend, companion
lūdō, 3, lūsī, lūsus. to amuse oneself, jest, joke
8 The sense of this line is: quī dē amōre scītis.
9 **mēstō** (medieval Latin form): **maestus, -a, -um.** sad, unhappy
parcō, 3, pepercī, parsus. to spare (+ dative)

Translation of French line
10 great is my grief

11 **attamen** (conjunction, = at tamen). but nevertheless
consulō, 3, consuluī, consultus. give thought to, look after (+ dative)

Translation of French lines
12 by your honor
14 makes me weep a thousand tears

15 **pectus, -oris** N. breast, heart

Translation of French line
16 to remedy me

17 **fierem.** In medieval Latin the imperfect subjunctive is used in less vivid conditions.

Translation of French line
18 by a kiss.

COUR D'AMOUR

16. DIES, NOX ET OMNIA

Diēs, nox et omnia
michi sunt contrāria,
virginum colloquia
   me fay planszer,
oy suvenz suspirer,
   plu me fay temer.

O soldālēs, lūdite,
vōs quī scītis, dīcite,
michi mēstō parcite,
   grand ey dolur,
attamen consulite
   per voster honur.

Tua pulchra faciēs,
mē fay planszer miliēs,
pectus habet glaciēs;
   a remender,
statim vīvus fierem
   per un baser.

Day and night, night and day,
all the world besets me —
the lovely laughter of young girls
makes me melt into a pool of tears.
I am pining, longing, full of fears.

My friends mock me, taunt me!
O call me what you please!
You should spare me lost in loving
and give me advice for your
   honour's sake.

O, your lovely face
makes me shed a thousand tears
for your heart is hard as ice.
A single kiss from your lips
would make me live again!

The lover presents his beloved with a bouquet of lilies and roses symbolizing her purity and his love. This illustration is an example of manuscript illumination, in which the artist painted his illustration directly on the manuscript. The colors of these illuminations were usually very bright and vivid and gold was often lavishly used for extra richness. (Illustration from Benedictbeuern ms.)

According to the conventions of courtly love, woman was to be highly honoured and respected by man. Any man who fell in love with her had to love her from afar, until he proved himself worthy of her regard and, ultimately, of her love. This he could do by performing brave deeds in her name, by honouring her in poetry and song, and by being humbly obedient to her slightest wish or command. A true knight was not just a brave hero, but a man who was inspired by his love for a lady to serve her in all ways. Love, by these courtly conventions, was not solely a personal, private emotion, but an emotion of high honour which affected every aspect of one's actions, public and private.

The *carmina* in the section "Cour d'Amour" trace the love affair between the woman and man of *carmina* 15 and 16, as we shall see. Do these *carmina* form a pair? The man and the woman love each other; yet they are lonely and sad. In the words of *carmen* 4 they are both *volvuntur in rota*, being kept apart by these courtly conventions. Orff has arranged the music for these two *carmina* to represent aurally the emotions of the two lovers. Do the melodies of these two *carmina* express happiness or sadness? Are the melodies smooth and even, or jerky and "tortured"?

VOCABULARY

1 **puella, -ae** F. girl, maiden
2 **rūfus, -a, -um.** red
   tunica, -ae F. tunic; dress
4 **crepō, 1, crepuī, crepitus.** to make a thin, soft noise; rustle
7 **tamquam** (adverb). just like
   rosula, -ae F. rosebud
8 **faciē.** ablative of respect
   splendeō, 2, splenduī, ---. to shine, be bright
9 **ōs, ōris** N. mouth, face

17. STETIT PUELLA

Stetit puella		There she stood,
rufā tunicā;		a young girl
sī quis eam tetigit,		in a scarlet dress.
tunica crepuit.		If anyone touched it,
		it rustled!
Eia.	5	Eia!
Stetit puella,		There she stood,
tamquam rosula,		a young girl
fāciē splenduit,		like a rosebud.
ōs eius flōruit.		Her face glorious,
		her mouth a blossom!
Eia.	10	Eia!

In his *De Arte Honeste Amandi,* Andreas stated that "Love is a kind of innate suffering which is born out of the vision of and continual recollection of the beauty of the person of the opposite sex." Are we to think of this *carmen* as the picture the man has of his beloved which he continually recollects in her absence? Or are we to think of him as suddenly coming upon a woman whose beauty overwhelms him, so much that he hardly seems able to approach her; at most perhaps someone (*si quis*) -- but not he himself -- might just touch her garment?

"My love is like a red, red rose," said Robert Burns, the great romantic Scottish poet. To what flower does our poet compare this woman? The language of this *carmen* -- for instance the words *rosula, splenduit, floruit* -- should remind you of the *carmina* in the section "Primo Vere." To judge from these words would you say the man admires the woman or idolizes her as though she were a goddess, perhaps the goddess of spring herself?

Orff's music reinforces the picture of the man so caught up in contemplation of his beloved that he is unable to notice anything else. Orchestral accompaniment is at a minimum; the instruments play a very simple melody *pianissimo*. Our attention is focused on the words of the soloist. Contrary to one's expectations, the soloist, however, is a woman! Orff has once again scored his *carmen* in a surprising way, for the soprano represents Venus who is "charming" the man into love through this *carmen*. From what Latin word is our English word "charm" derived?

VOCABULARY

1. **circā** (preposition). around, about (+ accusative)
2. **suspīrium, -ī** N. sigh, sighing
3. **pulchritūdō, -inis** F. loveliness, beauty
4. **quê** (medieval Latin form): **quae.** The antecedent is suspiria.
   lêdunt (medieval Latin form): **laedō, 3, laesī, laesus.** to harm, hurt

Translation of German lines
5. Manda liet
6. manda liet
7. my darling
8. does not come.

(The meaning of "manda liet" is unknown.)

9. **lūceō, 2, lūxī, ---.** to shine, glow
10. **radius, -ī** M. ray, beam
11. **splendor, -ōris** M. flash, gleam
    fulgur, fulguris N. lightning bolt
12. **dōnō, 1.** to give
    tenebrae, -ārum F. shadow, darkness

Translation of German lines
13. Manda liet
14. manda liet
15. my darling
16. does not come

18. CIRCA MEA PECTORA

Circā mea pectora
multa sunt suspīria
dē tuā pulchritūdine,
quē mē lēdunt miserē.
    Manda liet,
    manda liet,
    min geselle
    chumet niet.

Tuī lūcent oculī
sīcut sōlis radiī
sīcut splendor fulguris
lūcem dōnat tenebrīs.
    Manda liet,
    manda liet,
    min geselle
    chumet niet.

My heart is filled
   with sighing;
Your face is as fair
   as my grief is great.
    Manda liet,
    Manda liet,
    My love
    does not come.

Your eyes' glance is
   as bright as the sun,
As lightning flashing
   in the dark of night.
    Manda liet,
    Manda liet,
    My love,
    does not come.

VOCABULARY, continued

17   **volō, velle, voluī, ---.** to grant

      The two imperfect subjunctives, together with the pluperfect subjunctive in line 20, would, in classical Latin, describe a wish unfulfilled in present time. In this instance, however, they seem simply to express a wish and are being used as equivalents of present subjunctives: "May God grant, may the gods grant ..."

18   **prōpōnō, 3, -posuī, -positus.** to propose, put forth

19   **virgineus, -a, -um.** virginal, maidenly

20   **reserāssem = reservāvissem**

Translation of German lines

21   Manda liet
22   manda liet
23   my darling
24   does not come.

18. CIRCA MEA PECTORA, continued

Vellet deus, vellent dii,		May God, may the gods
quod mente próposui:		grant me my dearest wish,
ut eius virginea		To unlock the bonds
reserássem vincula.	20	of her virginity!
Manda liet,		Manda liet,
manda liet,		Manda liet,
min geselle		My love
chumet niet.		does not come.

The maiden finds her reflection of more interest than her lover and his *sodales*, but Cupid will soon change her indifference into love. The instruments include the lute, two recorders, and a harp. The recorder, a kind of "beaked" flute, had six fingerholes and a thumbhole enabling it to span two octaves and a note. It was a popular instrument from the eleventh to the eighteenth centuries. Originating in the Near East in the third millenium B.C., the harp spread all over Europe. Perhaps the favorite instrument in the middle ages, it is still the national instrument of Ireland.

Carmen 18 is divided between a baritone singing a "groaning" line of melody and a chorus singing a German refrain. Our lover is unhappy as his words *suspiria* and *misere* show, but he has gathered up enough courage to address his plea for love to the "goddess" of *carmen* 17. Note his words *tua* (line 3) and *tui* (line 9). What words of his plea correspond to the description of the beautiful woman in *carmen* 17?

In *carmen* 16 our lover asked his *sodales* to cease mocking him for his failure as a lover and give him some sympathy and advice on how to win her heart. Are we to think of the chorus here in *carmen* 18 as his *sodales*? If so, is the chorus mocking him or sympathizing with him?

In stanza 3 our lover ceases to beg for his lady's love; it would seem she has disdainfully turned away. To what deity (deities) is he praying?

VOCABULARY

1 **puellula, -ae** F. little girl. The diminutive expresses endearment.

2 **morārētur:** The imperfect or present subjunctive in medieval Latin may be used in future less vivid conditions.

cellula, -ae F. little room

3 **coniunctiō, -ōnis** F. union, meeting
Esset should be supplied in this line.

4 **suscrescō, 3, -crēvī, -crētum.** to rise, increase

5 **pariter** (adverb). equally, evenly on both sides

medium, -ī N. middle

6 **prōpellō, 3, -pulī, -pulsus.** to drive out, cast out

tēdium (medieval Latin form): **taedium, -ī** N. weariness, tiredness

7 **lūdus, -ī,** M. pleasure, delight

ineffābilis, -e. inexpressible, indescribable

8 **membrum, -ī** N. limb

lacertus, -ī M. muscle

labium, -ī N. lip, mouth

19. SI PUER CUM PUELLULA

Sī puer cum puellulā
morārētur in cellulā,
   fēlix coniunctiō.

Amōre suscrescente,
   pariter ē mediō
prōpulsō procul tēdiō,
fit lūdus ineffābilis
membrīs, lacertīs, labiīs.

If a boy and a girl
tarry in seclusion,
   happy is their union!

As their love grows —
   both his and hers —
   all shame disappears!

Pleasure indescribable —
arms, breasts, lips!

A frequent trysting-place was the garden which, with its hedges and mazes, gave lovers some privacy. This French woodcut dates from about 1500. (From G. Whicher, *The Goliard Poets*; see Bibliography.)

According to Orff's directions, six men of the chorus (three tenors, a baritone, and two basses) sing this little *carmen*. The verbs are in the subjunctive mood, and, according to the grammar of medieval Latin, we should view the lines of this *carmen* as an expanded future less vivid condition. This *carmen*, then, does not describe an actual meeting between two lovers, but fantasizes about such a meeting, expressing what was in the lover's mind as he sung lines 17-20 of *carmen* 18. Recall Andreas' explanation of the origin of love on page 92; what do you suppose is the role of such fantasizing in courtly love?

This *carmen* also emphasizes a common theme in poems of courtly love: the kiss, a symbolic act of union. Even today, the kiss of the bride and groom at the end of the marriage ceremony symbolizes their union in marriage. The courtly lover consequently dwells much, in his meditation, upon kissing or his beloved's mouth. What lines in the *carmina* of this section, "Cour d'Amour," are also concerned with the mouth or lips of the beloved?

VOCABULARY

1. **veniō, 4, vēnī, ventum, venī**: imperative; **veniās**: subjunctive expressing a wish
2. **nē...faciās.** negative command

   morior, 3, mortuus sum. to die, perish
3. The meaning of lines 3-4 is unknown.
5. The construction of lines 5-8 is: pulchra (est) faciēs...et aciēs...et seriēs.
6. **aciēs, -ēī** F. glance, look
7. **capillī, -ōrum** M. hair

   seriēs, ---. F. braiding, arrangement (genitive not found)
8. **clārus, -a, -um.** beautiful, lovely

   quam clāra speciēs! how beautiful! how lovely a sight!
9. **rosa, -ae** F. rose. **rosā**: ablative of comparison
   The construction is: (tu es) rosā rubicundior.

   rubicundus, -a, -um. rosy, red
10. **līlium, -ī** N. lily

    candidus, -a, -um. white, fair
11. *__formōsus, -a, -um.__ beautiful, pretty
12. **glōrior, 1, -ātus sum.** to glory in, take pride in

20. VENI, VENI, VENIAS

Venī, venī, veniās,
nē mē morī faciās,
hyrca, hyrce, nazaza,
    trillirivos...

Pulchra tibi faciēs,   5
oculōrum aciēs,
capillōrum seriēs,
ō quam clāra speciēs!

Rosā rubicundior,
līliō candidior,   10
omnibus formōsior,
semper in tē glōrior!

Come, come, oh, please do come!
Don't make me die of longing!
  Hyrca, hyrce, nazaza
    trillirivos!

Beautiful your face,
  your eyes,
  your hair!
Oh, how beautiful you are!

Redder than the rose,
Whiter than the lily!
  Most beautiful of all,
  always in you will I glory!

The lute was a common instrument of the Goliards. It had a large body shaped like half a pear and a long fretted neck usually bent at a sharp angle just below the peg box. It was played by plucking the strings. An Arabic instrument (l'ud, "the piece of wood"), the lute was brought to Europe during the Islamic conquests of Spain. (Illustration from J. Harter, *Music: A Pictoral Archive of Woodcuts and Engravings,* Dover Publications Inc., New York: 1980.)

Certain themes common to poems of courtly love which we have seen in the previous *carmina* are repeated in *carmen* 20. What lines express the themes of the woman's aloofness and the idealization of the woman? Note also the last two lines of the *carmen*. This theme of boasting will be picked up in a later poem.

What is the effect of the change from the imperative *veni* to the optative subjunctive *venias* in line 1?

In *carmen* 19, the increasing intensity of passion is shown by the increasing swiftness of tempo. Why, do you suppose, did Orff write a double choral arrangement for *carmen* 20, since it is a very passionate and very personal plea of man to woman?

VOCABULARY

1. **trutina, -ae** F. balance (of a pair of scales)
   dubius, -a, -um. wavering, vacillating
2. **fluctuō, 1,** to rise and fall, flow back and forth
3. **lascīvus, -a, -um.** shameless, wanton
   pudīcitia, -ae F. modesty. Both amor and pudicitia are modified by contraria; the feminine adjective form is chosen for the sake of rhyme.
4. **ēligō, 3, -lēgī, -lectus.** to choose, select, elect
5. **collum, -ī** N. neck
   prēbeō (medieval Latin form): **praebeō, 2, -buī, -bitus.** to offer, submit (+ dative)
6. **transeō, -īre, -iī, -itus.** to go under, submit

21. IN TRUTINA

In trutinā mentis dubia
   fluctuant contrāria
lascīvus amor et pudīcitia.
   Sed ēligō quod videō,
   collum iugō prebeō;   5

ad iugum tamen suāve
   transeō.

On Hesitation's balance am I
   suspended,
   pulled   asunder
by wanton love   and Modesty.
   But
I choose what I see before me,
I offer myself to Love's subjection.
   To that sweet slavery I go!

According to the rules of courtly love, as given by Andreas, love was a service or submission (*servitium*). The lover was bound to obey all his lady's commands, just as a vassal was bound to obey his lord. The lady, however, also had to follow rules prescribing her behavior. She was to test her lover for humility, courtesy, and faithfulness. While she should not award her regard easily, once she had made an adequate testing of his character and love, she was bound to accept him as her lover. In short, while she was free to choose among men, she was not allowed to abuse this freedom. In this *carmen*, is love seen as a submission and a service? By whom to whom?

In the previous *carmina*, reading between the lines, we may understand that the woman has been testing her lover for his faithfulness and devotion; now, making her decision, she is hesitating still. Love (*amor*) and chastity (*pudicitia*) are warring within her. Are you surprised that she describes love as *lascivus*? After all, her society valued love very highly. Andreas states that "Love is the fountain and spring of all good things" and that "All agree that there is nothing that is good in the world and no civility of society that does not flow forth from love."

Love, however, could exist only between those unmarried to each other. The Countess Marie, Andreas says, even decided that if two lovers married, their continuing love was wicked (*nefandus*)! Thus, essentially, "proper" love could only be adulterous or illicit, but even Andreas seems to feel some need to justify this self-contradiction. He argues that the bestowal of love must first be given freely and, for it to redound to the man's credit (since he must win it), love should be given only by a woman superior to him. Since, Andreas says, a wife owes her husband affection, this affection cannot be called "love"; furthermore, the husband is superior to the wife, who must obey him, and thus she cannot honor him by bestowing her love upon him. Such concepts of love opposed completely all ecclesiastical teachings on love and chastity, and it is no wonder that the lady of *carmen* 21 wavers in indecision.

Orff's music expresses her indecision: does the melodic line flow evenly, or would you characterize it as wavering?

VOCABULARY

1 **tempus, -oris** N. time; season, time of the year
   iocundus, -a, -um. pleasing, delightful
3 **congaudeō, 2, -gavīsus sum.** to delight, rejoice
7 **iam** (adverb). now
   virginālis, -e. of a maiden, girl
8 **ardeō, 2, arsi, ---.** to burn, be on fire
11 **confortō, 1.** to please, delight
12 **prōmissiō, -iōnis** F. yielding
13 **dēportō, 1.** to displease, make sorry, grieve
14 **negātiō, -iōnis** F. refusal, denial, rejection
21 **brumālis, -e.** wintery, of winter
22 **patiens, patientis.** quiet, inactive
23 **animus, -ī** M. breath, spirit
   vernālis, -e. of spring
24 Supply **est** in this line.

22. TEMPUS EST IOCUNDUM

Tempus est iocundum,
  ō virginēs,
modo congaudēte
  vōs iuvenēs.

Oh, oh, oh,
  tōtus flōreō,
iam amōre virgināli
  tōtus ardeō,
novus, novus amor
  est, quō pereō.

Mea mē confortat
  prōmissiō,
mea mē deportat
  negātiō.

Oh, oh, oh,
  tōtus flōreō,
iam amōre virgināli
tōtus ardeō,
novus, novus amor
  est, quō pereō.

Tempore brumālī
  vir patiens,
animō vernālī
  lascīviēns.

Welcome is spring
  to you, sweet lasses!
Now rejoice,
  you young lovers!

Oh, oh, oh,
I am abloom with love!
Now with love for a girl
am I all ablaze!
This is a new, new love
I am dying of!

Each small yielding
  makes me yield the more,
My modest refusal
  brings me only pain.

Oh, oh, oh,
I am abloom with love!
Now with love for a girl
am I all ablaze!
This is a new, new love
I am dying of!

In winter's cold
  a man's blood runs cool,
But it rushes hot
  at spring's warm breath.

VOCABULARY, *continued*

31 **lūdō, 3, lūsī, lūsus.** to tease; entice, lure on
32 **virginitās, -ātis** F. virginity
33 **dētrūdō, 3, -trūsī, -trūsus.** to push away, drive away
34 **simplicitās, -ātis** F. innocence, ingenuousness
41 **domicella, -ae** F. little mistress

22. TEMPUS EST IOCUNDUM, continued

Oh, oh, oh,
   tōtus flōreō,
iam amōre virgināli
   tōtus ardeō,
novus, novus amor
   est, quō pereō.

Mea mēcum lūdit
   virginitās,
mea mē dētrūdit
   simplicitās.

Oh, oh, oh,
   tōtus flōreō,
iam amōre virgināli
   tōtus ardeō,
novus, novus amor
   est, quō pereō.

Venī, domicella,
   cum gaudiō,
venī, venī, pulchra,
   iam pereō.

Oh, oh, oh,
   tōtus flōreō,
iam amōre virgināli
   tōtus ardeō,
novus, novus amor
   est, quō pereō.

25 Oh, oh, oh,
   I am abloom with love!
Now with love for a girl
   am I all ablaze!
This is a new, new love
30   I am dying of!

My maidenhood
   cheats me,
But my innocence
   holds me back.

35 Oh, oh, oh,
   I am abloom with love!
Now with love for a girl
   am I all ablaze!
This is a new, new love
40   I am dying of!

Come, my mistress,
   come with joy,
Come, come, my beauty,
   for I am dying!

45 Oh, oh, oh,
   I am abloom with love!
Now with love for a girl
   am I all ablaze!
This is a new, new love
50   I am dying of!

The frequent plagues of the middle ages, and particularly the Black Death, which killed an estimated 25,000,000 between 1247-1350, contributed to the preoccupation of the medieval mind with death and the decay of the body. The morbid concept of the "Dance of Death" originated in a late thirteenth century poem, and soon church walls and psalters showed grinning skeletons grabbing shuddering partners from among the living. The Dance of Death was even performed as a pantomime in Paris in 1422 with men dressed as skeletons partnering figures clothed to represent every rank of society. (Illustration from E. V. Gillon, Jr., *The Middle Ages,* Dover Publications Inc., New York: 1971. Original from A. Schramm, *Der Bilderschmuck der Frühdrucke,* K. W. Hiersemann, Leipzig.)

The words *tempus est iocundum* refer to spring and remind us of *carmina* 3, 4, and 5 in which the poets bid young men and women to rejoice. *Floreo* is an important word in the refrain of this *carmen*. It, too, provides a link to earlier *carmina*. In what other *carmina* do words with the base *flor-* appear? Which *carmen* in "Primo Vere" contains words related to *brumalis* and *lasciviens*?

Certain themes of the other *carmina* in "Cour d'Amour" appear in this *carmen*. What lines here express the themes of the aloof woman, of man her vassal, of the idealization of woman, of the conflict between courtly love and Christian morality?

VOCABULARY

1 **dulcis, -e.** sweet
2 **subdō,** 3, **didī, -ditus.** to submit, yield

23. DULCISSIME

Dulcissime,
tōtam tibi subdō mē!

My sweetest love,
I give myself to you!

In *carmen* 22 the woman was hesitating to accept the man as her lover, though he had performed the *servitium* courtly love demanded. Now the roles are reversed, and she enters into *servitium*, or submission to him.

The orchestration for *carmina* 22 and 23 forms a single unit of exciting music and rapid tempo representing audially the passion of the lovers. The stanzas are divided between a baritone, soprano (*carmen* 23), and choruses of boys, women, men, and a "super chorus" of all three. Notice carefully how the stanzas are divided among the soloists and the choruses, since these stanzas reveal the attitudes towards love of the lover, his lady, and medieval society in general. If the choruses of women and men, respectively, represent "all women" and "all men", what is the attitude of the women's chorus towards love in lines 11-14 of *carmen* 22? Are these attitudes similar to the men's attitudes towards love in lines 21-24? When Orff unites both choruses for lines 41-44, is he implying that the attitudes of men and women may be initially different, but come into agreement later?

Let us look more closely at the attitudes of the lover and his lady. The man has finished his long submission or *servitium* of love towards his lady. With her acceptance of him, the relationship of love now finally exists between them. Hence he talks of *novus amor*. Would you say that the man is still as humble towards his lady as he was in *carmen* 18, or is he, rather, proud and boastful to have gained her love? Note that the woman also sings the *totus floreo* stanza (lines 25-30). Does this imply that her attitude towards love is now identical to the man's? His last comment on love comes when he repeats the *totus floreo* stanza (lines 45-50). Her last comment is *carmen* 23. Has her attitude changed or is her attitude towards love more complex than the man's?

Lastly, note that the phrase *iam amore virginali* in line 7 is sung by the man and in line 17 by the woman. Is it possible for this Latin phrase to mean two different things when sung by two different people? Can you think of a translation which uses the same words but ambiguously means two different things?

VOCABULARY

1 **avē!** hail!
2 **gemma, -ae** F. jewel, gem
  pretiōsus, -a, -um. precious, valuable
3 **decus, -oris** N. glory, pride, ornament
4 **glōriōsus, -a, -um.** glorious, splendid
5 **lūminār, -āris** N. light, lamp
7 **Blanziflōr, -is** F. Blanchefleur, heroine in a thirteenth century romance
  Helena, -ae F. Helen of Troy, wife of Menelaus, king of Sparta
8 **generōsus, -a, -um.** of noble birth, noble-spirited

BLANZIFLOR ET HELENA

24. AVE FORMOSISSIMA

Avē formōsissima,
   gemma pretiōsa,
avē decus virginum,
   virgō glōriōsa,
avē mundī lūminār,
   avē mundī rosa,
Blanziflōr et Helena,
   Venus generōsa!

Hail most beautiful,
   gem most precious,
Hail pride of virgins,
   glorious Virgin,
Hail Light of the World
   Hail Rose of the World
Blanziflor and Helena,
   Peerless Venus!

Like certain of the other *carmina, carmen* 24 is a parody of a Christian hymn. A clue to which particular kind of hymn is being parodied is given by the word *"Ave"*. Who is hailed with *"Ave"*? What woman is regarded by the Church as *decus virginum* and *luminar mundi*? Another title of hers is *"lilium"*, the lily, called *"blanchefleur"* in French. The white lily symbolizes purity and chastity, while the red rose symbolizes fidelity or constancy, and is also another symbol of the Virgin Mary. These flowers are appropriate in an ironical way for this woman who has just been wooed and won by her lover. In what other *carmina* has she been described by floral imagery?

Lines 7-8 refer to a famous heroine of medieval romance. Blanziflor, or Blanchefleur, to give the French spelling of her name, was the daughter of a Christian slave. She was raised from childhood with Flore, the son of the king of Spain, who was a Saracen, one of an Arabic tribe who had conquered most of Spain. At age 15, while Flore was away, Blanchefleur was sold to a slave merchant. When Flore heard this, he set out to find her and traced her to the harem of an emir of Babylon. Though Flore was discovered and caught before he could save her, the judges, before whom the two lovers were brought, were touched by their loyalty. They allowed the two to marry and return to Spain where Flore converted all his people to Christianity.

Though Blanchefleur, or Blanziflor, through her purity and loyalty to Flore, can rightly be held up as a model for women, the second epithet, Helena, is ironically used. Helena, though unfaithful to her husband, was regarded as a model for women by the Goliards because she submitted herself to the commands of Venus and eloped with Paris. The Goliard poet honors the woman who is the subject of this *carmen* with the title *Venus generosa* because her yielding to his love has brought him, also, supreme happiness.

Orff subtitles this *carmen* "Blanziflor et Helena". It is a hymn of honor to a maiden who has given herself totally to love. This *carmen* declares that love has, in the words of *carmen* 8, ennobled her to such an extent that she has become equal to two of the heroines of medieval romance, equal, even, to Venus herself. In the eyes of her lover, and of the Goliards, she can rise no further.

Regno.

BIBLIOTHECA
REGIA
MONACENSIS

regnabo

regnavi

sum sine regno.

F. VI. Hesas ambulante pastu sere peri. pro
digus non recipit uitium auari. iuxus comparati
quadam singulari debet medium ad utrumque unum
extute contemplari. Si legisse memoras editam ca
tonis. in qua scriptum legitur: ambula cum bonis.
cui ad dandi gloriam animum disponis. inter cete
in hoc primum consideri. quis sit dignus donis. Dare

FORTUNA IMPERATRIX MUNDI

25. O FORTUNA

   Ō Fortūna
      velut lūna
   statū variābilis,
      semper crescis
      aut dēcrescis;   5
   vīta dētestābilis
      nunc obdūrat
      et tunc cūrat
   lūdō mentis aciem;
      egestātem,   10
      potestātem
   dissolvit ut glaciem.

      Sors immānis,
      et inānis
   rota tu volūbilis,   15
      status malus,
      vānā salūs

O Fortune, like the moon
you are always changing,
waxing now, now waning,
never the same for long remaining.
How can we love this hateful life
which pampers us, then harries us,
bemusing and confusing us,
always in temper humorous —
   poverty, prosperity,
dissolving both as sun does ice?

O Luck, ill of nature, ill of will,
you spin us round at dizzy rate,
carrying us to high estate,
then to ruin, your heart obdurate.
Your profitless prosperity like mist

25. O FORTUNA, *continued*

semper dissolūbilis,
    obumbrāta
    et vēlāta   20
michi quoque nīteris
    nunc per lūdum
    dorsum nūdum
ferō tuī sceleris.

    Sors salūtis   25
    et virtūtis
michi nunc contrāria,
    est affectus
    et dēfectus
semper in angāriā.   30
    Hāc in hōrā
    sine morā
corde pulsum tangite;
    quod per sortem
    sternit fortem   35
mēcum omnēs plangite.

dissolving, then again us involving,
future veiling, us assailing,
grace and salvation denying.
    To Fortune's blows
    I bare my back.

O Luck, you ruin my health and strength,
robbing me of all confidence;
I bless your presence,
curse your absence,
living my life in painful hesitance.
Let us all mourn together
For in this very hour
Fortune shows her power!
    Fortune in her whimsy
    overwhelms the brave.

Carmen 25 is *carmen* 1 repeated, and like it, is placed in its own section; if *carmen* 1 is prologue, *carmen* 25 is epilogue. Its mood is a complete constrast to the glorious happiness of *carmen* 24. In determining the meaning or function of *carmen* 25 as an epilogue we must consider what links, in theme(s) or vocabulary, it has with the other *carmina*.

One of the prominent themes of these *carmina* is that of love and man's relationship to it and to its goddess, Venus. Love brings men and women their greatest happiness, honor, and glory. Love, says the poet of *carmen* 8, ennobles one, and *carmen* 24 is a hymn in honor of the woman who has yielded herself to love in obedience to Venus' commands. To show, metaphorically, the bliss the lover enjoys, the poet of *carmen* 3 depicts a god and goddess in love. This poem also initiates a symbolic association between love, flowers, and blessed happiness: the lover is both *beatus* and *elatus*, two key words used to describe the one whom Fortuna favors in *carmen* 2. Thus, in making *carmen* 25 an epilogue, Orff is comparing the powers of Venus and Fortune. This epilogue warns us not to accept unreservedly the view of love presented by the Goliards: one should not blindly obey Venus as the poet of *carmen* 5 urges as he sings, *"Simus iussu Cypridis gloriantes et letantes pares esse Paridis."* This last word, *Paridis,* is one of several references to the Trojan War made throughout Orff's selections. Recall the other *carmina* which refer to participants in this war. In one, Hecuba was held up as a monitory emblem of Fortuna's power. Hecuba was, in a sense, overthrown by the actions of the lovers, Helena and Paris. What we may conclude about love and life from Orff's ending is discussed in the following section.

FORTUNA IMPERATRIX MUNDI

Of all the ancient divinities, only Fortuna survived through the change in religion that occurred when Christianity became the dominant religion of the Roman Empire. Why she was able to do so is a complicated question to answer. Part of the answer lies in the fact that she was not a deity with a specialized function or sphere of influence. She was an omnipotent deity, like Jupiter, whom she supplanted as supreme pagan god. Her survival after the advent of Christianity also lies in the collapse of the Roman Empire, which seemed to portend for Christians the increasing disorder and conflict which was to herald the Second Coming of the Lord. The breakdown of Roman society and government, together with the sudden, unpredictable invasions and calamities of the fifth and sixth centuries A.D., showed Fortuna to be an entity increasingly active in the world, and the unpredictability of her character became more and more pronounced.

No one could influence her, let alone control her. She respected not rank, not wealth, not merit. She favored the good and bad equally, and abandoned them with equal disregard to their deserts. The despair expressed by *carmen* 1 was an emotion readily understood by medieval men and women, who surely, in weeping for the speaker, wept for themselves. That Orff chose to have a chorus sing this *carmen* shows his recognition of the universality of this theme to the medieval mind.

Fortuna's character is mysterious; not only do men's fortunes wax and wane, but even her power over the world seems to wax and wane, viewed from man's standpoint. Thus she is like the moon, which waxes and wanes. *Carmen* 1 abounds with contrasts which describe her power: *crescis aut decrescis, obdurat et curat, egestatem potestatem, immanis et inanis, est affectus et defectus*. Truly she is *obumbrata et velata*, obscure and cloaked as to her presence, intent, and effect. Controlling all, a natural force as immanent in the universe as heat and cold, she is rightly called by Orff *Imperatrix Mundi*.

Surely then, she is the major character of Orff's *Carmina Burana*. Yet in the sections "Primo Vere," and in "Cour d'Amour," Venus appears as the ruling deity. Upon those who follow her commands to love, Venus, not Fortuna, bestows honor and happiness. This apparent contradiction as to their relative importance and influence in the world becomes more puzzling when one looks at the *carmina* of "In Taberna," which intervene between the two sections just mentioned. In the Taberna *carmina*, Venus is mentioned only once, and as for Fortuna, she is not mentioned at all by name, though a synonym of hers, *sors*, occurs in *carmen* 13. Who then is the main subject of the *Carmina Burana*? Who is truly the *Imperatrix Mundi*? And what is the thematic structure of Orff's opus?

Since Orff calls her *Imperatrix Mundi*, Fortuna must be the main character. That she does not appear to be so, in the main sections of the opus is due to her character: the ambiguity inherent in her character effects the ambiguity of the thematic structure of the whole work.

Her character is clearly described in *carmen* 1: she is *variabilis, obumbrata, velata* in purpose and action. Her apparent blessings may be in reality losses, and vice versa. She is the *sors salutis et virtutis*, two words which are ambiguous, having pagan and Christian meanings. *Salus* can mean mundane prosperity, i.e. riches and power, but also, in the Christian sense, spiritual prosperity: from the latter notion develops the word "salvation." *Virtus* can mean, in pagan terms, worth, power, excellence, strength; to a Christian it means virtue, moral excellence. Which meanings, pagan or Christian, do the words have here? Or are both meanings implied? Already Fortuna's ambiguity is clear!

Carmen 2, however, clarifies the meanings of *salus* and *virtus*. Fortuna bestows *munera, prosperitas, gloria, felicitas*. The one favored by her is *felix et elatus* and, like a king, is crowned, with flowers. The floral imagery, however, is used ironically. Flowers last but a season, and then wither: they metaphorically suggest that the happiness Fortuna gives is as ephemeral. Fortuna gives worldly prosperity only to take it away as she did from Hecuba.

The floral imagery is an important thematic link between *carmen* 2 and the other sections of Orff's work. The imagery of the fortunate one flourishing (*florui*), crowned with flowers (*flore coronatus*) is reiterated in the *carmina* of "Primo Vere." In *carmen* 3 Phoebus is covered with flowers as he reclines in Flora's lap and even though it is Venus (through Flora) who crowns the devoted lover, Phoebus, the floral motif still carries with it the associations of *felicitas* and *beatitas* given to it in *carmen* 2. Though the subsequent *carmina* do not employ so expressly the floral motif as this picture in *carmen* 3, yet the equation has been established: flowers = love = divine happiness. The floral motif is used in other ways as well. Flowers set the scene for spring and describe the physical charms of the loved one, *e.g. suzer rosenvarwer munt* (*carmen* 9). This latter use of the floral motif reappears in *carmina* 17, 20, and 24, and so links the section "Primo Vere" with "Cour d'Amour." Other linking motifs between these two sections are Cupid (*carmina* 4, 5, and 15) and the antithesis between winter: frozen emotion :: spring : awakened emotion (*carmina* 3, 4, 5, 7, and 16 and 22).

Yet if there is a single major theme of the *carmina* of "Primo Vere," it is that of Venus' supremacy. We are ordered to obey Venus' commands to love, to praise her for the happiness she bestows through this love and for the glory and honor this love gives the beloved. The culminating picture of "Primo Vere" is that of the supreme glorification love can bring. As the singer of *carmen* 8 states, love is ennobling, and the poet of *carmen* 10 would indeed lose the whole world for love and count it gain.

From this zenith of human happiness we fall to the nadir, or so it seems, as we begin the section "In Taberna." The mood and tone of this section contrasts diametrically with the blithe and merry mood of "Primo Vere." In tone and arrangement these *carmina* are more akin to *carmina* 1 and 2. Orff has, however, scored *carmina* 11-14 as three solos (for the most part) and a chorus, and this scoring contrasts them to the two opening *carmina*. *Carmina* 1 and 2 are solo statements of Fortuna's power sung by a chorus to emphasize the universality of Fortuna's power over men. *Carmina* 11-13 are solos scored as solos to personalize the helplessness of man in life: he is like a boat without a pilot, a bird buffeted by the wind, a swan trussed up. When Orff changes the score from solo to chorus as he does for part of *carmen* 13, his scoring emphasizes the universality of man's helpless condition.

But before whom is man so helpless? In overt imagery and language there appears only one mention of Venus, in *carmen* 11. Again she appears as a pleasure-giving goddess, but the singer seems to lack the joy expressed by the *carmina* of "Primo Vere." Her connection with the despair and hopelessness of the poet of *carmen* 11 is unclear. For surely if he has obeyed Venus, he should be feeling as exalted as the lovers in "Primo Vere."

Hidden among the words of *carmen* 11 are clues as to the direction the whole opus is taking. Here reappear the key words of *carmen* 1, *salus* and *virtus*. Which meaning, pagan or Christian, do they have now? In stanzas two and three occur similes drawn from the Gospels, which should indicate that the Christian meanings of *salus* and *virtus* are implied. Stanza two is a clear reference to the parable of the wise man building his house upon a rock. In stanza three the skipperless ship out of control recalls the incident in *Matt.* 14.23-33, where the disciples, sailing across the lake without Jesus, were storm-tossed; when Jesus appeared walking on the water, the storm was calmed and the disciples were saved. Though it seems clear that the Christian meaning of *salus* and *virtus* are to be understood here in *carmen* 11, it is still unclear exactly what this implies for their use in *carmen* 1 and what these words have to do with Venus.

As a further complexity, there is in this section no overt, clear mention of Fortuna, by name, though she seems to be addressed by a synonym, *sors*, in *carmen* 13. The choral scoring of this part is significant, for it reminds us of the omnipotent Fortuna, bestowing pain and loss, as described in *carmina* 1 and 2.

Carmina 12-14 further mystify the direction and total meaning of the opus at this point. All they appear to have in common is that they are drinking songs, but in topic and theme they seem unrelated to each other and to all the other *carmina*. Yet there exists a relationship, obscured though it may be. The weird *carmen* 12 is a metaphor of a soul roasting in Hell. A key word in "Cour d'Amour," *pulcher* (*carmina* 16, 18, 20 and by implication 24), occurs in this *carmen*. *Carmen* 13 may be taken as a comment on the vanity of worldly pleasures; they are ephemeral, easily lost. *Carmen* 14 is scored significantly as a chorus to emphasize the universality of its theme, and of the themes of the whole section. Not only are worldly pleasures ephemeral, but they are empty ones; pleasure itself becomes a frantic, never-ending pursuit. The picture of everyone aimlessly and constantly drinking is hellish, for would it not be Hell to have to do one thing constantly and forever, so that even pleasure becomes a torture?

With the opening of "Cour d'Amour," we return to the mood of "Primo Vere," where there exists love, and loving youths and maidens, and happiness. The only sadness occurs when Venus has not yet provided a lover; here *carmen* 15 parallels *carmen* 7. As the *carmina* unfold, we find that they tell the story of a love affair. The floral imagery, especially that of the rose, and the metaphor of the icy heart not yet warmed by love harken back to that earlier section. The difference is that these *carmina* are highly personal, and in this resemble *carmen* 11. Slowly the image of the beloved one is painted before our eyes in *carmina* 17, 18, and 20, culminating in the first utterance of the beloved woman who has finally been touched with love. In her soliloquy she vacillates between *pudicitia* and *lascivus amor*, two concepts with definitely moral, Christian overtones. Having made her decision to follow Venus' commands, she calls her service *suave*, the same word the poet of *carmen* 11 used to describe his service to Venus. This word makes an ironic link between the two *carmina*. The poet of *carmen* 11 seems to have gotten little pleasure and certainly not permanent pleasure from his service to Venus. What will be the final reward for this young woman, who decides to serve Venus?

Finally, of all the *carmina* in "Cour d'Amour," the language of *carmen* 22 is the most reminiscent of "Primo Vere" as the following list shows:

Primo Vere	**carmen 22**
Flore, floret, flore	*floreo*
gaudia, gaudere	*gaudeo, congaudete*
iocundus	*iocundum*
ver	*tempus iocundum*
hyemis	*tempus brumale*
lascivit	*lasciviens*

Clearly then the *carmina* of "Primo Vere" and "Cour d'Amour" are linked in tone, subject, imagery, and language. If they may be reduced to one theme, it is the glorification of love, that is, service to Venus which brings supreme joy, felicity, and honor. But what links the "In Taberna" *carmina* to the other sections of the opus? There are the words *salus, suave* and *virtus* (*carmen* 11) and a brief mention of Venus as ruling deity, but such links seem tenuous, slight, and shadowy.

Carmina 24 and 25, however, resolve the ambiguity of connection and ultimate theme of the opus. *Carmen* 24, which, like *carmen* 10, serves as the culmination of its section, has as its topic the apotheosis of the woman who is totally obedient to Venus. The woman who has yielded herself to love is compared to Venus, in fact is Venus on earth. In parallel to this pagan imagery, she is hailed as another Mary, the glory of Christian womanhood, through the titles of the Virgin. In this poem the conflict between the pagan and Christian ethics is most acute, since the poet, in equating the woman to both Mary and Venus, essentially equates them to each other. At the same time, the *carmen* is supremely ironical, since the woman is hailed as *virgo gloriosa* and *decus virginum* at the very moment she has ceased to be a virgin.

Carmen 25 finally ends the conflict in themes and structure of the opus. It foretells that the woman so apotheosized, so crowned with flowers, the metaphor of love and glorification through love, will experience quickly a downfall. To Fortuna it is all a game, a *ludus*. The very word *ludus* should recall to us the other occurrences of the word. One is in *carmen* 11, where the poet is like a leaf *de quo ludent venti*. The metaphor of life as a game is continued in *carmina* 13 and 14 in which gambling plays so large a part. There is also the *ludus* of love, described in *carmen* 19. Love, and life, are games, but who is the gamester, who the dice? In error man thinks he is the player, but it is Fortuna who plays and he is her marker. Having brought him to his downfall, she begins again on a new toy. For that reason the opus concludes with *carmen* 1 again: the opus has come full circle, as it were. Even now as the chorus sings its warning, someone is, with hope, riding on the upward swing of Fortuna's wheel. Thus Fortuna, not Venus, is the final disposer of man's fate. Fortuna, not Venus, is *Imperatrix Mundi*.

If Fortuna is *Imperatrix Mundi*, what is her relationship to God, the supreme governor of the universe? If she is independent of Him, He is not omnipotent. If she is subservient to Him, in what way is she *Imperatrix*?

Boethius, a Roman philosopher and statesman of the sixth century A.D., tried to resolve this theological impasse which was not a mere logical problem for him, but a personal one. Imprisoned unjustly at Pavia and ultimately condemned to death, he wrote the *De Consolatione Philosophiae* to explain why good, and bad, men do not receive their just desserts. He concluded that all fortune, whether harsh or kind, come to reward and employ the good or to punish and correct the bad; in the case of the latter, even bad fortune is "good," since it chastises the erring soul and directs it towards its ultimate redemption. In his own case, he has lost ephemeral, worldly pleasures, but has retained the good fortune of redemption through Christ. Everything that is good proceeds ultimately from God, and Boethius sees Fortuna, whether she is kind or harsh, as working to bring forth good in every situation, through God's providence (*Cons. Phil.* 4 *PR*.6 and 7, 5 *pr.* 1).

Medieval theologians developed Boethius' solution of making Fortuna one of God's chief servants. Perhaps Dante (1265-1321) was, after Boethius, most responsible for the Christianization of Fortuna. In a famous passage in the seventh canto of *The Inferno*, Vergil explains to Dante Fortuna's true role in God's scheme, a role, the Roman philosopher-poet states, which is commonly misunderstood by men. Just as He created the angels to guide the celestial phenomena, so God created Fortuna to guide the Earth's splendors. To the extent that she is above men, as the angels are, human reason cannot totally comprehend her or her actions and she appears to be *obumbrata et velata* to it. Other medieval authors, such as Chaucer and Chrestien de Troyes, followed Dante in making Fortuna one of God's servants. Orff, also, follows Dante: he calls Fortuna *Imperatrix Mundi*, Ruler of the Earth.

Created by God to be his minister on earth, to reward the good, and particularly to punish and chastise the bad in this life, so that they might serve as a warning to the rest of mankind, Fortuna emphasizes her lessons by heaping honor upon honor, wealth upon wealth, on anyone deserving punishment and then by suddenly bereaving him of all. So the sinner would learn not to seek or value any transient honor or prize of beauty, sexual love, or glory, but turn his mind to seek God, virtue, and salvation. Of all the seven deadly sins -- Lust, Pride, Gluttony, Envy, Anger, Sloth, Covetousness -- the deadliest is Pride, because it is the mental attitude of consciously or unconsciously comparing oneself to God. For the sin of Pride Lucifer was banished from Heaven to reign in Hell.

"Pride goeth before destruction, and a haughty spirit before a fall." (*Proverbs* 16.18). Fortuna is especially the agent of punishment for Pride. Appropriately then Orff concludes his opus with *carmina* 14 and 25. The former is the apotheosis of the woman who has chosen Lust (Venus), not *Pudicitia*, and prides herself on the glory she thereby wins. Rolling upwards on Fortuna's wheel, compared to Venus and Mary, Queen of Heaven, she in her splendor epitomizes Pride before its fall. The latter *carmen* asserts Fortuna's role of *Imperatrix Mundi*, punisher of the sinner and servant of God. Through imaginative use of music, chorus, and soloists Orff has shaped his *Carmina Burana* into a medieval morality play.

The average medieval man perhaps did not fully understand, as Vergil pointed out to Dante, that in Fortuna's mad caprices lay God's method for directing men to His worship and service. Certainly, however, the average medieval man saw her as a personage to be reckoned with. As variable in appearance as in her purpose and actions, Fortuna appears in many illuminations of manuscripts, woodcuts, and paintings. She is often shown as being two-faced, one face frowning. If she is depicted single-faced, the artist represents the duality of good and bad fortune by making one half of her face white, the other black. She may have wings, for Fortuna is fleeting; she may be blind-folded, or even blind, since she seems not to regard merit in handing out rewards or ruin. Often she has only a forelock of hair and is bald on her head to show how difficult it is to snatch at Fortune. This image of her goes back to a statue sculpted by the Greek artist Lysippos (?365-?320 B.C.), who thus portrayed *Occasio* (Chance). Fortuna's clothing, also, may be of varying hue.

Varying, too, are the epithets medieval poets give her. The Italians called her, among other things, *fallace* (deceitful) and *favorvole* (favor-flightly). The French addressed her as *cruelle* (cruel) and *belle* (beautiful). By English poets she is termed blind and double (double-dealing). Writers of medieval Latin verse described her as *amara* (bitter), *fera* (untamed), and of course, *volubilis* (changeable).

Many a medieval poem exists which mentions her, as is fitting, since the average man saw her as being in full control of his life. In many illustrations she is shown standing on a ball which symbolizes both the earth, over which she rules, and her inherent instability. Most commonly, however, she is shown standing near a wheel which she turns. The wheel is perpendicular to the ground and below it, usually, is a deep pit or grave. The wheel also is a symbol of Fortuna's fickleness and instability and has its origins in classical notions of Fortuna; so Seneca writes in the *Agamemnon* 71-72: *ut praecipites regum casus Fortuna rotat!*

The various stages in which Fortuna favors and then abandons man are shown in reference to the wheel. Men, standing in line, approach it, waiting their turn for Fortuna's favor. One has begun to climb onto the wheel, ready to take his chance at success, fame, and fortune. Sometimes a whole series of men, clothed as merchants, nobles, or bishops, are strapped to the wheel; sometimes only four men are shown with little inscriptions indicating their relationship to Fortuna. The man at the top of the wheel ususally holds a sceptre and wears a crown: his inscription reads *"Regno."* To his right, a figure falling from the wheel grabs at his crown as it slips from his head; his inscription reads *"Regnavi."* At the bottom of the wheel, stretched out, bereft of crown and sceptre, is the figure titled *Sum sine regno."* On the wheel's left, a man is climbing up, undaunted by the fate of the last two figures; he is described as *"Regnabo."*

Fortuna continues her reign in man's imagination even today. In casinos at Las Vegas, Atlantic City, and elsewhere, gamblers continue to call upon her in the words of a popular song from the musical *Guys and Dolls:* "Luck, be a lady tonight!"

CARL ORFF

Born in Munich, July 10, 1895, Carl Orff was both a composer and a musical educationist. After graduating from the Munich Academy of Music in 1914, he served as Chorus Master at the Munich Kammerspiele, at the Mannheim Nationaltheater, and at the Darmstadt Landestheatre, before returning again to Munich in 1919 to begin teaching. Five years later he joined Dorothee Gunther in founding the Guntherschule for music, gymnastics, and dance. Through his work he has changed worldwide the practices of elementary music education. Basically his theory draws upon the forms of vocal expression children naturally use. The contents of his *Musik für Kinder* (preliminary exercises, folksongs, dance-tunes, and improvised structures) have been translated into English, Welsh, Japanese, Greek, and Portuguese, as well as into many other languages. Such arrangements underlie the folk idioms in many cultures, and Orff's educational use of them is another aspect of his concern and fascination with old material, whether it be folklore, fairy tales, legends, or literature from times past. Orff himself once said, "I am often asked why I nearly always select old material, fairy tales and legends for my stage works. I do not look upon them as old, but rather as valid material. The time element disappears, and only the spiritual power remains. My entire interest is in the expression of spiritual realities. I write for the theatre in order to convey a spiritual attitude."

Besides basing three of his works on Greek plays by Aeschylus and Euripides, Orff utilized in his various compositions elements of Christmas and Easter plays and Monteverdi's baroque operas. His style of composition, nonetheless, is not complex, but direct and simple, and the *Carmina Burana* perhaps is the best example of it. Rhythm is the most striking feature of Orff's music, and it is simple rhythm. Very rarely is there any counter-rhythm. Consequently the attention of the audience is centered on the words, since there are no distracting instrumental variations or flourishes. Neither did Orff make much use of polyphony; his music resembles that of plainsong rather than the complicated melodies in the sonatas, symphonies, fugues, and symphonic poems of Bach, Mozart, and Beethoven. Though he admired these composers greatly, Orff believed that they themselves exhausted the possibilities of these forms of music. He preferred to turn his attention to the spoken word and the musical stage.

Consequently all the fugues, sonatas, and other formal pieces of music he wrote before 1935, Orff withdrew from public domain or destroyed. In 1935 he began composing the *Carmina Burana* which was produced in 1937 in Frankfurt am Main, and on this and his subsequent musical dramas on classical and metaphysical subjects his fame and popularity rests. His major stage works and their sources are as follows: from ancient authors, *Antigone, Catulli Carmina, Trionfo di Afrodite, Oedipus der Tyrann, Prometheus;* from Bavarian folklore, *Die Bernauerin, Astutuli;* from fairy tales and legends, *Der Mond, Der Kluge;* from medieval and renaissance sources, *Carmina Burana, Ein Sommernachtstraum, Ariadne, Orpheus, Tanz der Spröden, Comoedia de Christi resurrectione, Ludus de nato infante mirificus, De temporum fine comoedia.*

Carl Orff died March 29, 1982.

MEDIEVAL LATIN

The Latin which was spoken and written by Cicero was highly regarded by subsequent writers who consequently imitated his style and expression. The average Roman spoke, and wrote, a Latin different from this "educated" Latin in grammar, spelling, and vocabulary. As different nationalities were absorbed into the Roman Empire, new words were brought into Latin, new pronunciations of Latin occurred, and the grammar was not always mastered. We have some examples of this linguistic change in Petronius, while other examples are found in the epitaphs inscribed on tombstones found in all parts of the Empire.

With the advent of Christianity many new words came into Latin. Latin is a language concrete in expression, and words for the abstract concepts of philosophical and religious argument were mostly lacking. Words for these concepts were often borrowed from Greek, or new Latin words, which were very literal translations of Greek words, were invented. *Ecclesia* and *monachos* are examples of transliterative borrowing, *personalis* and *essentia* are examples of translative borrowing.

At first, of course, Christian writing was entirely in Greek; St. Paul even wrote to the Church at Rome in Greek. The first Latin Christian writing was a translation of the Bible, which used not "classical" or Ciceronian Latin, but the Latin of the *vulgus*, the common people of the provinces. This translation, made around the end of the second century A.D., was redone by St. Jerome in the late fourth century. His Latin reflects the vulgar Latin of the common people, but also uses many Graecisms and Hebraisms since he knew both languages. Since he had studied Latin at Rome under Donatus, certain elements of "classical" Latin also appear in his work.

St. Jerome's Latin is representative of ecclesiastical Latin which is the basis for the medieval Latin of the *Carmina Burana*. The major points on which medieval Latin differs from classical Latin are as follows:

1. Greater use of abstract and compound nouns, and of diminutives and of words transliterated from the Greek.
2. Change of gender in nouns.
3. An extended use of prepositions where classical Latin uses case alone.
4. The general disappearance of the periodic sentence with its many dependent clauses.

5. The disappearance, to a great extent, of indirect statement.
6. The substitution of the Greek indirect statement construction in which indirect statements are introduced by conjunctions.
7. The extension of this construction to purpose and result clauses.
8. The use of the infinitive to express purpose or result (another Greek construction) and indirect commands.
9. The use of the subjunctive where classical Latin does not, and vice versa.
10. Greater use of periphrastic verbs.
11. Changes in spelling.

Recordings Presently Available

Carmina Burana. Armstrong, English, Allen, Previn, London Symphony and Chorus. ANGEL S-37117 (Q)

Carmina Burana. Auger, Van Kestern, Summers, Muti, Philharmonia Orchestra and Chorus. ANGEL SZ-37666

Carmina Burana. Blegen, Riegel, Binder, Thomas, Cleveland Orchestra and Chorus. COLUMBIA M-33172

Carmina Burana. Casapietra, Hiestermann, Stryczek, Kegel, Leipzig Radio Symphony and Chorus. PHILHARMONIC 9500040

Carmina Burana. Harsanyi, Petrak, Presnell, Ormandy, Philadelphia Symphony, Rutgers Choir. COLUMBIA MS-6163

Carmina Burana. Hendricks, Aler, Hagegard, Mata, London Symphony and Chorus. BCA ATC 1-3925

Carmina Burana. Janowitz, Fischer-Dieskau, Stolze, Jochum, Berlin Opera Orchestra and Chorus. DG139362

Carmina Burana. Mandac, Kolk, Milnes, Ozawa, Boston Symphony, New England Conservatory Chorus. RCA LSC-3161

Carmina Burana. Popp, Unger, Fruehbeck de Burgos, Stowkowski, Houston Symphony. ANGEL S-36333; SERAPHIM S-60236

Carmina Burana. Subrtova, Tomansk, Srubar, Smetacek, Czech Philharmonia and Chorus. QUIN 7122

Carmina Burana. Vulpius, Rotzch, Rehm, Kegel, Leipzig Radio Orchestra and Chorus. DG 2535275

Current recordings are listed in the current *Schwann Catalogue,* available at any radio and phonograph store.

Ray Manzarek, *Carmina Burana.* Produced by Philip Glass and Kurt Munkacsi. 1983. A&M RECORDS, INC.

BIBLIOGRAPHY

W. Beare, *Latin Verse and European Song*. Methuen: London 1957

J. Bridgeman. *Wine, Women, and Song: Selections from the Carmina Burana*. American Classical League: Oxford OH 1984

F. Brittain, *Medieval Latin and Romance Lyric to A.D. 1300*. Cambridge University Press: Cambridge 1951

P. Dronke, *Medieval Latin and The Rise of European Love Lyric*. 2 vols. Oxford University Press: Oxford 1968

F. Goldin, ed., *Lyrics of the Troubadours and Trouveres*. Garden City: Doubleday 1973

C.S. Lewis, *The Allegory of Love*. Oxford University Press: Oxford 1936

H.R. Patch, *The Goddess Fortuna*. Harvard University Press: Cambridge MA 1927

J. Stevens, *Medieval Romance: Themes and Approaches*. Norton: New York 1973

G.F Whicher, *The Goliard Poets*. Harvard University Press: Cambridge MA 1949

J.J. Wilhelm, *The Cruelest Month: Spring, Nature and Love in Classical and Medieval Lyrics*. Yale University Press: New Haven 1965

VOCABULARY

ā, ab (prep. with abl.) from, away from; by
abbas, abbatis M. abbot
absum, -esse, āfuī, āfutūrus. to be away, be absent
aciēs, aciēī F. acuteness, sharpness; power; glance, look
ad (prep. with acc.). to, toward; near
adiungō, 3, -iunxī, -iunctus. to join with, associate with (+ dative)
aegrōtus, -a, -um. sick, ill
āēr, āeris N. air
aestās, aestātis F. summer
aestuō, 1. to burn
affectus, -ūs M. eagerness, zeal; attention
agō, 3, ēgī, actus. to do; act; drive; treat
albus, -a, -um. white
alter, altera, alterum. the other of two
altus, -a, -um. high; deep
amābilis, -e. likeable; lovable; pleasant
amāritūdō, -inis F. bitterness; despair
amārus, -a, -um. bitter; sorrowful
amīcus, -ī M. friend; lover
amō, 1. to love
amoenus, -a, -um. pleasant
amor, amōris M. love
ancilla, -ae F. maidservant
angāria, -ae F. forced service; tribulation; struggle
anima, -ae F. soul, spirit
animus, -ī M. mind; courage
antīquus, -a, -um. former
anus, ūs F. old woman
Aprīlis, -is M. April
ardeō, 2, arsī, ---. to burn; take on fire
attamen (conj.). but, nevertheless
auctōritās, -ātis F. authority, influence
audiō, 4, -īvī, -ītus. to hear
auferō, -ferre, abstulī, ablātus. to take away, steal
aut (conj.). or
avē (interjection). hail!
avidus, -a, -um. greedy (+ gen.)
avis, avis F. bird
axis, axis M. axle of a wheel
Bacchus, -ī M. Bacchus, the god of wine
beātus, -a, -um. fortunate, blessed
bibō, 3, bibī, ---. to drink

143

VOCABULARY

bibulus, -ī M. a drinker
Blanziflōr, -is F. Blanchefleur, heroine of a medieval romance
bravium, -ī M. prize, reward
brūma, -ae F. winter
brūmālis, -e. of winter, wintery
calvātus, -a, -um. bald
candidus, -a, -um. white; fair
canticum, -ī N. song
cantō, 1. to sing
cantus, -ūs M. song
cānus, -a, -um. grey-haired, white-haired; old
capillātus, -a, -um. having long hair
capillus, -ī M. hair
capiō, 3, **cēpī, captus.** to take, capture
captīvus, -ī M. captive
careō, 2, **caruī, ---.** to lack, miss (+ abl.)
caveō, 2, **cāvī, cautus.** to be on one's guard against, beware of
cēdō, 3, **cessī, cessus.** to go, go away; give way, yield
celebrō, 1. to celebrate, hymn, honor in song
celer, celeris, celere. swift, quick
cellula, -ae F. little room
centum (indeclinable adj.). one hundred
certātim (adverb). in rivalry, competition
cēterus, -a, -um. the rest, the remaining
chorus, -ī M. chorus
Chrīstiānus, -ī M. a Christian
cignus, -ī M. swan
cinis, cineris M. ashes
circā (prep. with acc.). around, about
clāmō, 1. to shout
clārus, -a, -um. beautiful, lovely
clāvis, -is F. door-key
clērus, -ī M. clerk, minor church official
coetus, -ūs M. flock
colloquium, -ī N. voice; conversation
collum, -ī N. neck
colō, 3, **coluī, cultus.** to live in, dwell in, inhabit
comparō, 1. to compare, to liken to
cōnfortō, 1. to please, delight
cōnfundō, 3, **-fūdī, -fūsus.** to confound, throw into disorder
congaudeō, 2, **-gāvīsus sum.** to delight in, rejoice
coniūnctiō, -iōnis F. union; meeting
coniungō, 3, **-iūnxī, -iūnctus.** to join together, unite
cōnor, 1. to try, strive, contest

VOCABULARY

consilium, -i N. deliberation; counsel; council, senate; church council
constans, -antis. settled, stay-at-home
consulo, 3, -sului, -sultus. to give thought to, look after (+ dative)
contrarius, -a, -um. contrary, opposed to (+ dative)
cor, cordis N. heart; feeling
coronatus, -a, -um. crowned
corruo, 3, -rui, ---. to fall, tumble, sink
crepo, 1, crepui, crepitus. to rustle, make a thin, soft noise
cresco, 3, crevi, cretum. to grow, increase, wax
Cucaniensis, -is M. Cockaigne, Cucany, a make-believe land of the Goliards
cum (conj.). since; although; when
cum (prep. with abl.). with
cunctus, -a, -um. all
Cupido, -inis M. Cupid, the god of love
cura, -ae F. care
curo, 1. to take care of, tend, treat, pamper; to care for, take heed of, be mindful of
curro, 3, cucurri, cursus. to run, race; compete
custodia, -ae F. place for safe-keeping; custody
cutis, -is F. skin
Cypris, -idis F. Venus, the goddess of love
cytharizo, 1. to play the cithara; sing
dapifer, -i M. servant, waiter
de (prep. with abl.). from, down from; concerning, about; with
decanus, -i M. deacon
decies (adverb). ten times
Decius, -i M. P. Decius Subulo, a man infamous for his dissolute life
decresco, 3, -crevi, -cretum. to grow smaller, decrease, wane
decus, decoris N. glory; pride; ornament
defectus, -us M. failure; absence
defunctus, -a, -um. dead, deceased
dens, dentis M. tooth
denudo, 1. to strip bare, strip naked
deporto, 1. to displease; make sorry, grieve
descendo, 3, -scendi, -scensum. to fall, sink
detestabilis, -e. abominable, execrable, detestable
detrudo, 3, -trusi, -trusus. to push away, drive away
deus, -i M. god
dextera, -ae F. right hand; pledge, contract; friendship
dico, 3, dixi, dictus. to say, tell
dies, -ei F. day
discordo, 1. to be at odds with someone, be angry at someone
dispersus, -a, -um. scattered, dispersed
dissolubilis, -e. dissolvable, destroyable

VOCABULARY

dissolvō, 3, -solvī, -solūtus. to loosen, separate, destroy
dō, dare, dedī, datus. to give
domicella, -ae F. little mistress
dōnō, 1. to give
dorsum. -ī N. back
dubius, -a, -um. wavering
dulcēdō, -inis F. sweetness
dulcis, -e. sweet, pleasing
dulcisonus, -a, -um. sweet-sounding, pleasantly-ringing
dum (conj.). while, until
duodeciēs (adverb). twelve times
dūrō, 1. to last, last out; suffice
ē, ex (prep. with abl.). out of
ecce (interjection). lo!, behold!
efferō, -ferre, extulī, ēlātus. to carry out; spread abroad; lift up, elate
egens, egentis. poor, needy
egestās -ātis F. poverty, want
ego (pronoun). I
ēgredior, 3, -gressus sum. to go out
ēlātus, -a, -um. exalted; lofty, high
elementum, -ī N. element
ēligō, 3, -lēgī, -lectus. to choose, select; elect
enim (conj.). for, indeed
equitō, 1. to ride on horseback
et (conj.). and
exaltō, 1. to exalt, raise
extō, 1. to stand forth, be prominent or conspicuous
exul, exulis M. exile, banished person
faciēs,-ēī F. face
faciō, 3, fēcī, factus. to make; do
fava, -ae F. honey-comb
fēlix, fēlicis. happy; blessed, fortunate
ferō, ferre, tulī, lātus. to bring, carry, bear; endure
fidēlis, -e. faithful; believing
fidēliter (adverb). faithfully
fidēs, -ēī F. faith, trust
fiō, fiērī, factus sum. to be made, be done; become; happen
Flōra, -ae F. Flora, goddess of flowers and spring
flōreō, 2, -uī, ---. to bloom, blossom; flourish
flōs, flōris M. flower, blossom
fluctuō, 1. to rise and fall, flow back and forth
fluvium, -ī N. river
folium, -ī N. leaf
formōsus, -a, -um. beautiful, pretty
fortis, -e. brave
fortiter (adverb). very much, strongly

VOCABULARY

Fortúna, -ae F. Fortune, the goddess of luck
fráter, -tris M. brother
frendō, 3, frenduī, ---. to gnash, grind
frons, frontis F. front, forehead
fugiō, 3, fūgī, fugitum. to flee
fugō, 1. to put to flight, drive away
fulgur, fulguris N. lightning bolt
fundámentum, -ī N. foundation of house or dwelling
fundō, 3, fūdī, fūsus. to stretch, extend
garcifer, -ī M. boy; servant
gaudeō, 2, gāvīsus sum. to rejoice
gaudium, -ī N. joy
gemma, -ae F. jewel, gem
generōsus, -a, -um. of noble birth, noble-spirited
gens, gentis F. tribe, group of people
gerō, 3, gessī, gestus. to carry; wage, carry on.
      cúram gerere (+ genitive) to take care of
girō, 1. to turn on a spit
glaciēs, -ēī F. ice
glōria, -ae F. glory
glōrior, 1. to boast, brag, vaunt
glōriōsus, -a, -um. glorious, splendid
gradior, 3, gressus sum. to go, wander, rove, travel
grandō, -inis F. hail, hail-storm
grātus, -a, -um. pleasing; thankful
gravis, -e. heavy; severe; serious
gravitās, -ātis F. heaviness, seriousness
gremium, -ī N. lap
habitō, 1. to live, dwell in
Hecuba, -ae F. Hecuba, queen of Troy and wife of Priam
hēia (interjection). Oh!
Helena, -ae F. Helen or Helena, queen of Sparta, wife of Menelaus and lover of Paris
hera, -ae F. mistress of the house
herīlis, -e. of a man, man's
herus, -ī M. master of the house
hic, haec, hoc. this
hiemālis, -e. of winter, wintery
hiems, hiemis F. winter
hinc (adverb). from here, away
hōra, -ae F. hour
humus, -ī F. earth; grave, death
iaceō, 2, iacuī, ---. to lie, to rest
iam (adverb). already, now
iamiam (adverb). now
ibi (adverb). there, in that place

VOCABULARY

īdem, eadem, idem. same, the same
ignāvus, -a, -um. lazy, sluggish; cowardly; faint-hearted
ignōtus, -a, -um. unknown
ille, illa, illud. that
immānis, -e. monstrous; savage; horrible, inhuman
immemor, -is. unmindful, unheeding, disregarding (+ gen.)
immoderātē (adverb). freely, immoderately
imperātrix, -īcis F. she who rules, empress
imperō, 1. to command, order (+ dative)
in (prep. with abl.). in, on; (with acc.) into; against
inānis, -e. empty; unprofitable, worthless
indiscrētē (adverb). indiscreetly, shamelessly
induō, 3, -duī, -dūtus. to dress, clothe
ineffābilis, -e. inexpressible, indescribable
īnfimis, -a, -um. deepest, darkest
inplicō, 1. to grasp, embrace, entwine
insūdō, 1. to sweat (+ dative)
interius (adverb). inwardly, inside
intimus, -ī M. the inmost part
iocundus, -a, -um. pleasant, delightful; congenial
iocus, -ī M. joking, jesting
īra, -ae F. anger, rage
is, ea, id. this, that; (as pronoun) he, she, it
iste, ista, istud. that of yours
iter, itineris N. journey; march; road
iubeō, 2, iussī, iussus. to order, bid
iugum, -ī N. yoke; ridge
iustus, -a, -um. just, right
iuvencula, -ae F. young girl
iuvenis, -is M. youth, young man
iuventus, -ūtis F. youth, the prime of life
labium, -ī N. lip; mouth
lābor, lābī, lapsus sum. to slip, glide, flow
labor, -ōris M. toil, hardship
lacertus, -ī M. muscle
lacus, -ūs M. lake
laedō, 3, laesī, laesus. to harm, hurt
laetor, 1. to be glad, rejoice
laetus, -a, -um. glad, happy
lascīviō, 4, lascīvī, lascītum. to sport, frolic; be wanton
lascīvus, -a, -um. shameless, wanton
lātus, -a, -um. broad, wide
legō, 3, lēgī, lectus. to read
levis, -e. light, not heavy
lex, lēgis F. law; limit, moderation

VOCABULARY

libertīnus, -ī M. libertine, wastrel
libīdō, libīdinis F. desire
līlium, -ī N. lily
liquēscō, 3, licuī, ---. to melt
loquor, 3, locūtus sum. to speak, talk
lūceō, 2, lūxī, ---. to shine, glow
lūdō, 3, lūsī, lūsus. to play, frolic; gamble, play some game of chance
lūdus, -ī M. game, sport, past-time, joke; gambling game, dicing
lūminār, -āris N. light, lamp
lūna, -ae F. moon
lūx, lūcis F. light
maestus, -a, -um. sad, unhappy
magis (adverb). more
magus, -ī M. wise man, scholar
malus, -a, -um. bad, evil
māne (adverb). in the morning
māter, mātris F. mother
māteria, -ae F. material; timber
medium, -ī N. middle (of something)
mel, mellis N. honey
membrum, -ī N. limb
mēns, mentis F. mind
meritō (adverb). rightly, deservedly
mēta, -ae F. limit, end
meus, -a, -um. my, mine
mīles, mīlitis M. soldier
mīlle (indeclinable adj.). a thousand
mīllēnī, -ae, -a. thousands
minorātus, -a, -um. diminished, less
miser, misera, miserum. wretched, unhappy
miserē (adverb). wretchedly, sadly
mittō, 3, mīsī, missus. to send; throw, cast
modo (adverb). only; just now, lately
monachus, -ī M. monk
mora, -ae F. delay
moror, 1. to delay
morior, 3, mortuus sum. to die
mors, mortis F. death
mortuus, -a, -um. dead
mōs, mōris M. custom, habit; manner
multus, -a, -um. much
mundus, -ī M. world, earth
munus, muneris N. duty; gift
nam (conj.). for
nauta, -ae M. sailor

149

VOCABULARY

navigo, 1. to sail
navis, -is F. ship
nec, neque (conj.). and not, neither, nor
nectareus, -a, -um. fragrant, sweet-smelling
negatio, -ionis F. refusal, denial, rejection
nemus, -oris N. woods, forest
nequeo, 4, **-ivi, -itum.** to be unable
niger, nigra, nigrum, black
nimis (adverb). too much, overmuch
nitor, 3, **nisus sum.** to labor; press forward, attack (+ dative)
nix, nivis F. snow
nobilis, -e noble
non (adverb). not
nonies (adverb). nine times
noster, nostra, nostrum. our, ours
noto, 1. to note, mark
novitas, -atis F. newness, renewal
novus, -a, -um. new
nox, noctis F. night
nudus, -a, -um. nude, uncovered, bare
nullus, -a, -um. no, not one
nummata, -ae F. pennyworth
nummus, -i M. money
nunc (adverb). now
nunquam (adverb). never
o (interjection). oh!
obduro, 1. to harden, render hard
obumbratus, -a, -um. covered up, wrapped, enveloped
Occasio, -ionis F. the goddess Opportunity or Chance; another name for the goddess Fortuna
ocellus, -i M. eye
octies (adverb). eight times
oculus, -i M. eye
odor, -oris M. odor, scent, smell
olim (adverb). formerly, once
omnis, -e. all, every
optatus, -a, -um. desired, wished for, longed for
opus, operis N. work
os, oris N. mouth; face
paeniteo, 2, **-ui, ---.** to be penitent, repentent, sorrowful
papa, papae M. the Pope
par, paris. equal
Paris, -idis M. Paris, prince of Troy and lover of Helen, queen of Sparta
pariter (adverb). equally, evenly, on both sides
parum (adverb). hardly, scarcely

VOCABULARY

patiens, -ientis. quiet, inactive
patior, 3, passus sum. to suffer; allow, permit
pauper, -era, -erum. poor, penniless
pectus, -oris N. breast, heart
per (prep. with acc.). through
pereō 4, **-iī, -itum.** to perish, die
permaneō, 2, -sī, -sum. to remain, stay; last, continue
perversus, -a, -um. sinning, erring
petra, -ae F. rock, stone
philomēna, -ae F. nightingale
Phoebus, -ī M. Phoebus, the sun god
piger, pigra, pigrum. lazy, slothful, shiftless
pincerna, -ae M. butler
plangō, 3, -xī, -ctus. to lament, beat one's breast, bewail
plērumque (adverb). generally, usually, for the most part
pōnō, 3, posuī, positus. to put, place
post (prep. with acc. or abl.). after, behind
potestās, -ātis F. prosperity
praebeō, 2, -uī, -itus. to furnish; offer; show
praemium, -ī N. reward
praesentāliter (adverb). present
praesul, praesulis M. bishop
prātum, -ī N. field
prāvus, -a, -um. depraved, vicious
pretiōsus, -a, -um. precious, valuable
primus, -a, -um. first
principor, 1. to reign, rule
privātus, -a, -um. deprived of (+ abl.)
prō (prep. with abl.). before; for, in behalf of
probitās, -ātis F. correct behavior, honesty; sexual purity, virtue
procul (adverb). afar, at a distance
prōmissiō, -iōnis F. yielding, submission
prōmō, 3, prompsī, promptus. to bring forth, produce
propellō, 3, -pulī, -pulsus. to drive out, cast out
properō, 1. to hasten, rush
propinō, 1. to drink to a person by proposing a toast; to make a complimentary present of, to give as a token of honor; to serve, wait on a table
prōpōnō, 3, -posuī, -positus. to propose, put forth
proprius, -a, -um. right, proper, fitting
prosperitās, -ātis F. prosperity, riches
pudicitia, -ae F. modesty
puella, -ae F. girl, maiden
puellula, -ae F. little girl
puer, puerī M. boy

VOCABULARY

puerīlis, -e. boyish, childish; prankish
pulcher, -chra, -chrum. beautiful, lovely, handsome
pulchritūdō, -dinis F. loveliness, beauty
pulsus, -ūs M. beat, throb, stroke; beating of the heart, pulse
purpurātus, -a, -um. purple, rosy-purple
pūrus, -a, -um. pure
quaerō, 3, quaesīvī, quaesītus. to seek, ask; search
quam (adverb). how; (conj.). as, than
quamvīs (conj.). although
quandō (adverb). when
quater (adverb). four times
que (enclitic conj.). and
quī, quae, quod (relative pronoun). who, which; (interrogative pronoun) which, what
quīdam, quaedam, quoddam. a certain one
quīnquiēs (adverb). five times
quisquam, quaequam, quidquam. anyone, anything
quis, quid. (interrog. pronoun). who, what
quisquis, quaequae, quicquid (pronoun) and **quodquod** (adj.). whoever, whatever
quoque (adverb). also
radius, -ī M. ray, beam
rebellis, -e. always making war
recēdō, 3, -cessī, -cessum. to go back, recede
redeō, -īre, -iī, -itum. to come back, return
redūcō, 3, -dūxī, -ductus. to bring back, lead back
rēgina, -ae F. queen
regīrō, 1. to turn again and again on a spit
remōtus, -a, -um. far off, removed
rēs, reī F. thing, matter; affair, things in the world, nature; situation, plight
reserō, 1. to unlock, unclose, open
retineō, 2, -tinuī, -tentus. to retain, keep
rēx, rēgis M. king
rīdeō, 2, rīsī, rīsus. to smile, laugh
rīsus, -ūs M. laughter
rōdō, 3, rōsī, rōsus. to gnaw, backbite; complain; slander
rogus, -ī M. fire
rosa, -ae F. rose
rosulus, -ī M. rosebud
rota, -ae F. wheel
rubicundus, -a, -um. rosy, red
rudis, -e. rough; illiterate
rūfus, -a, -um. red
ruīna, -ae F. ruin, downfall
saccus, -ī M. sackcloth, rags

VOCABULARY

saevitia, -ae F. severity, harshness
saliō, 4, saluī, saltum. to leap, jump, hop
salūs, salūtis F. health; safety; welfare, prosperity; salvation
sapiēns, sapientis. wise, sagacious, provident
scelus, sceleris N. misfortune resulting from the ill-will of the gods; curse, affliction
sciō, 4, scīvī, scitus. to know
scrībō, 3, scrīpsī, scrīptus. to write; enroll, list
scutella, -ae F. salver, serving dish
secta, -ae F. sect, group
sed (conj.). but
sedeō, 2, sedī, sessum. to sit
sēdēs, -is F. place to sit, a seat; resting place; site
semel (adverb). once, once again
semper (adverb). always
septiēs (adverb). seven times
sequor, 3, secūtus sum. to go
serēnō, 1. to clear up, brighten, light up
serēnus, -a, -um. clear, bright, unclouded
seriēs, ---. F. braiding, arrangement
servus, -ī M. slave; servant
sexcentī, -ae, -a. six hundred; proverbially an infinite number
sexiēs (adverb). six times
sī (conj.). if
sīc (adverb). thus, so
sīcut (adverb). as if, just as
silva, -ae F. forest
silvānus, -a, -um. of a forest or woods; sylvan
similis, -e. like, similar
simplicitās, -ātis F. innocence, ingenuousness
sine (prep. with abl.). without
sīquis, sīqua, sīquid or **sīquod.** if any (man, woman, thing)
socius, -ī M. ally, associate; lover
sodālis, -is M. friend, companion
sōl, sōlis M. sun
solitus, -a, -um. usual, customary, accustomed
solium, -ī N. throne
sollemnis, -e. formal, obedient to laws of nature; solemn, ceremonial, festive
soror, -ōris F. lay sister
sors, sortis F. a lot, used in selection by chance; dice
speciēs, -ēī F. appearance, sight
spīrō, 1. to breathe, blow
splendeō, 2, splenduī, ---. to shine, be bright
splendor, -ōris M. flash, gleam

VOCABULARY

stō, 1, **stetī, status.** to stand
statim, (adverb). immediately
status, -ūs M. state, condition
sternō, 3, **strāvī, strātus.** to scatter, overthrow
stillō, 1. to drop, trickle, drip
stipō, 1. to crowd, surround
stultus, -a, -um. foolish, stupid
suāvis, -e. pleasant, sweet, attractive
sub (prep. with acc. and abl.). under; along
subdō, 3, **-didī, -ditus.** to submit, yield
subtīlis, -e. fine, nice, delicate
subtrahō, 3, **-trāxī, -tractus.** to take away, remove
sūgō, 3, **sūxī, suctus.** to suck
sum, esse, fuī, futūrum. to be
summus, -a, -um. highest, greatest
suprā (adv. and prep. with acc.). above; before
suscrescō, 3, **-crēvī, -crētum.** to rise, increase
suspīrium, -ī N. sigh, sighing
suus, -a, -um. his (own), her (own), its (own), their (own)
taberna, -ae F. tavern
taedium, -ī N. weariness, tiredness
tāliter (adverb). in such wise
tamen (conj.). nevertheless
tamquam (adverb). so as, just as, like as, alike, just like
tangō, 3, **tetigī, tactus.** to touch
tantus, -a, -um. so great, so much
temperō, 1. to regulate, rule
tempus, temporis N. time
tenebrae, -ārum F. shadow, darkness
teneō, 2, **tenuī, tentus.** to hold, keep
ter (adverb). thrice, three times
timeō, 2, **timuī,** ---. to fear
tollō, 3, **sustulī, sublātus.** to lift, raise; remove
tōtāliter (adverb). totally
tōtus, -a, -um. all, whole
trāmes, trāmitis M. path, course
transeō, 4, **-iī, -itus.** to go under, submit
tredeciēs (adverb). thirteen times
tristis, -e. sad, gloomy
trutina, -ae F. balance (of a pair of scales)
tū (pronoun). you (singular)
tunc (adverb). then
tunica, -ae F. tunic, dress
turpis, -e. ugly, foul; base
tuus, -a, -um. your, yours
ūber, -eris N. breast

VOCABULARY

ubi (adverb). where, in which place; when
undeciēs (adverb). eleven times
undique (adverb). from all sides; on all sides
ūrō, 3, ūssī, ustus. to burn, roast
ut (conj.) that; as, when; just as
ūtor, 3, ūsus sum. to use, enjoy (+ abl.)
vagus, -a, -um. roaming, flitting
vānus, -a, -um. empty; vain; unreliable, untrue
variābilis, -e. varying, variable, changeable
varius, -a, -um. colorful
vehemens, -mentis. violent, severe; furious
vēlātus, -a, -um. veiled, covered up, hidden
vēlox, vēlōcis. energetic, swift
velut, velutī (conj.). like
veniō, 4, vēnī, ---. to come
ventus, ī M. wind
Venus, Veneris F. Venus, goddess of love
vēr, vēris N. spring
vernālis, -e of spring
vertex, -ticis M. top, peak, summit
vērus, -a, -um. true
vespera, -ae F. evening
vestiō, 4, -iī, -ītus. to clothe, dress
vestis, -is M. clothing
vestītus, -ūs M. clothing
via, -ae F. road, way
videō, 2, vīdī, vīsus. to see; (passive) seem
vincō, 3, vīcī, victus. to conquer
vinculum, -ī N. chain, fetter, bond
vīnum, -ī N. wine
vir, virī M. man
virginālis, -e. of a girl, maidenly
virgineus, -a, -um. virginal, maidenly
virginitās, -ātis F. virginity
virgō, virginis F. girl, maiden
virtūs, -ūtis F. virtue; salvation
vīta, -ae F. life
vitium, -ī N. vice, corruption
vīvō, 3, vīxī, victum. to live
vīvus, -a, -um. alive, living
volitō, 1. to fly
volō, 1. to fly
volō, velle, voluī, ---. to wish, be willing
volūbilis, -e. spinning, revolving, turning
voluntās, -ātis F. wish, inclination
voluptās, -ātis F. pleasure, lust, debauchery

VOCABULARY

volvō, 3, **volvī, volūtus.** to turn, rotate (intransitive in passive)
vōs (pronoun). you (plural)
vulnus, vulneris N. wound
Zephyrus, -ī M. Zephyr, the west wind of spring

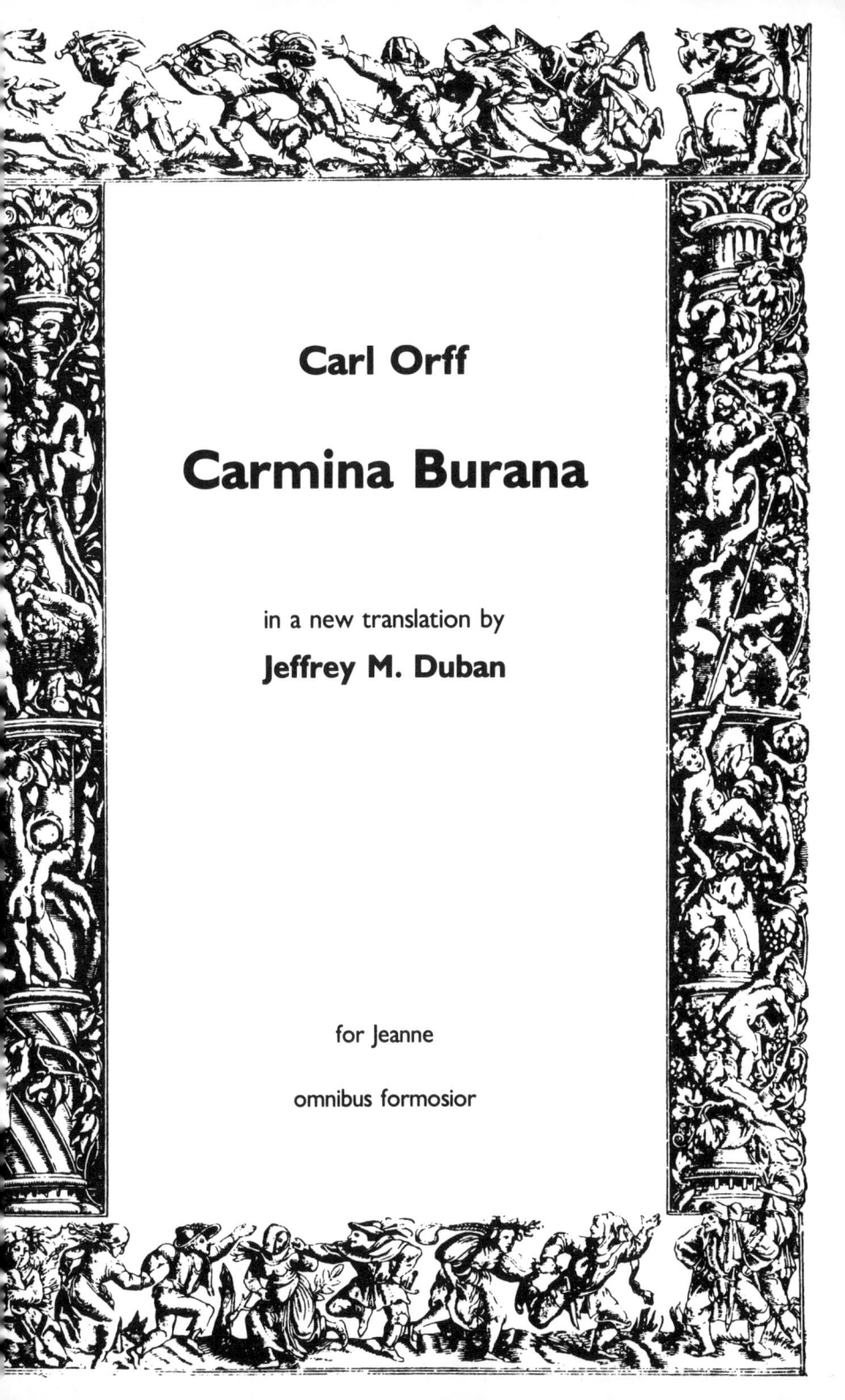

Carl Orff

Carmina Burana

in a new translation by
Jeffrey M. Duban

for Jeanne

omnibus formosior

TRANSLATION
INTRODUCTION
Fortune, Empress of the World

1. *O Fortuna* (Chorus)

O Fortune like the moon,
  you ever wane
  but to regain
  your former circumstance;
life's equally fain
  to decimate
  as reenstate
the mind with games of chance,
  prosperity
  and penury
reversing with a glance.

Immense and futile fate,
  uneasy ground
  safety unsound
mistakenly awaited,
to your wheel I'm bound;
  you've hidden your face
  denied your grace,
for sorrow was I slated,
  I've lost the knack
  this barren back
shows what you've perpetrated.

Unknown to me remain
  salvation's lot,
  of virtue aught;
equally loss and gain
await the hangman's knot.
  This very hour
  fails my power,
my pulse beats on the wane —
  fortune's a knave
  to impale the brave,
all weep now for my pain.

2. *Fortune plango vulnera* (Chorus)

Fortune's blow do I lament,
  my eyes, with weeping, red,
to find her favors but for rent
  and she, the harlot, fled.
True to form is her intent
  all riches to impart,
and then flee with your every cent
  and leave you there to smart.

Once I sat aloft, secure,
  on Lady Fortune's throne,
thinking her favors would endure,
  but now stripped to the bone.
Once was I full fatly grown,
  massaged and manicured,
My former self's now overthrown,
  my misery, assured.

Fortune's wheel slowly turns
  and leaves me sorely bowed,
since Fortune's warmth increasing burns
  the thoughtless overproud.
Let high seated potentates
  the wheel's script discern;
His royal person and his mate's
  collected in an urn.

PART I
In Springtime

3. *Veris leta facies* (Small Chorus)

Of Spring's fair-countenanced delight
  the world entire drinks,
harsh Winter's frost is put to flight,
  sharp ice recedes and shrinks.
In her gaily pied attire
  Flora now holds reign,
praised throughout the world entire
  in sweet-canticled refrain.

Steeped in flowers upon her breast,
  Phoebus, as befits the hour,
does laugh to find himself caressed
  by flower after flower.
Zephyr wafting from the West
  breathes fragrance through the bower —
O let us hasten Love's behest,
  concede his every power.

Now the tuneful nightingale
  trills forth her melody,
now the flower-resplendent vale
  revels in variety.
The winged flocks ascend the air
  throughout the pleasant lea,
there maidens' song abounds. There
  joy reigns all the day.

JEFFREY M. DUBAN

4. *Omnia sol temperat* (Baritone)

The sun rules over everything,
  piercing and delicate,
fresh April bids the world to sing
  of its renewed estate.
Young men's spirits are rallying,
  when thoughts are thus elated,
the boyish god is on the wing,
  let one and all be mated.

Spring's exalted renovation
  does everywhere reside,
Spring commands no jubilation
  excluded or denied.
When Spring embarks you on the wanton
  paths she has supplied,
see that your true and only one
  strays not from by your side.

So cherish me with all your heart,
  such is the love I feel,
no greater love could I impart,
  no truer love reveal.
Even times when we're apart
  your presence is no less real,
who loves, and loves with such a heart
  lies wracked upon the wheel.

5. *Ecce gratum* (Chorus)

  Anticipated
  variegated
Spring bursts into sight,
  long desired
  violet-fired
fields abound with light.
Let sorrows take to flight!
  Summer's heat
  marks the retreat
  Flee frost and snow
  away they go
together with the rest,
  Spring's growing thirst
  e'en now is nursed
at fragrant Summer's breast.
His life is dreariest
  who, in restraint
  resists, a saint
to Summer's warm behest.

They rejoice
  raise high their voice
In love's elated manner,
  whose foremost choice
  it is to hoist
Love's decorated banner.
Be Love then our commander —
  that we elated
  be equated
with princely Alexander.

On the Lawn

6. *Dance* (Orchestra)

7. *Floret silva nobilis*
  (Large and Small Chorus)

The noble woods bloom,
scent the air with perfume,
Ah, where shall I find
that old lover of mine?
He has galloped away —
who will love me, now, I say?

The forest blossoms far and wide
and I yearn for my lover.
When woods turn green on every side
will I my love recover?
He's left as fast as he can ride —
will I of all love be denied?

8. *Chramer, gip die varwe mir*
  (Soprano and Chorus)

Shopkeeper, please, a bit of pink
  my features to enhance,
  the more to make the young men
  think
sweet thoughts of gay romance.
  Look upon me
  young men
and be held in my trance!

Make love, good men
  and women all,
  answer love's ennobling call.
Flourish your felicity.
Hail, world, to thee,
  be joyed, I pray,
  my will is ever to obey,
accept your bounties day by day.

TRANSLATION

9. Round Dance (Orchestra) and
   Songs (Chorus)

Swaz hie gat umbe

Here are maidens in the round,
their dancing feet but touch the
  ground,
they'd like to go the Summer through
with lovers having nought to do!

Chume chum geselle min

Come, pretty maid of mine,
I wait for you, I pine,
I wait for you, I pine,
Come, pretty maid of mine.

Sweet rosy-colored mouth,
relieve me of my pain,
relieve me of my pain,
Sweet rosy-colored mouth.

10. *Were diu werlt alle min* (Chorus)

Were the world entire mine
from the ocean to the Rhine,
the whole of it would I forsake
that mighty England's queen awake
in my arms intertwined.

PART II
In the Tavern

11. *Estuans interius* (Baritone)

Storming with indignation,
  afflicted past relief,
my sorrow lacks remission,
  I question all belief;
this my mortal element
  will one day come to grief,
plaything to the blustering winds,
  as brittle as a leaf.

When choosing a location,
  the wise man will select
a bedrock as foundation,
  his interests to protect,
but I, the fool, am washed along,
  in my own refuse wrecked,
a firm and solid footing
  I everywhere neglect.

To what then do I compare?
  to a skipperless craft,
to a bird tumbling through air
  blown away by the draft;
no chains are there to bind me,
  no keeper holds the key,
I seek such as remind me
  of my depravity.

I consider the troubled thought
  to sport *mal apropos,*
sweet dissolution is my lot,
  what better way to go?
What Venus bids her favorite rake
  (let dullards sleep the day)
I'll not disdain to undertake,
  a consummate roué.

The road abounds with ample vice;
  each will I sample twice.
Virtue's a chore I've no need for,
  I'll pay damnation's price.
To self-indulgence do I turn,
  salvation's promise spurn —
roast my soul, take Satan his toll,
  the flesh is my only concern.

12. *Olim lacus colueram*
    (Tenor and Male Chorus)

Once I lived by the river's tide,
formerly most glorified,
while as a swan I did abide —

  Alack, alack,
  now roasted black
  from side to side.

Slowly I'm turned by the Maître D,
I'm scorched as black as I can be,
garnished with slips of greenery —

  Alack, alack,
  now roasted black
  most piteously.

Here I lie upon the platter,
that once I flew now doesn't matter,
teeth now greet me at full clatter —

JEFFREY M. DUBAN

Alack, alack,
no turning back,
could anything be sadder?

13. *Ego sum abbas*
  (Baritone and Male Chorus)

I'm tavern abbot of Cucany,
with drinkers keep I company,
a gambler's is my pedigree.
Who seeks me for dice at early morn
will by night of shirt and shorts
  be shorn.
And thus denuded will he mourn;

Wafna, wafna!
O infamous fate, I am forlorn,
joy's former estate
is turned to scorn!

14. *In taberna quando sumus*
  (Male Chorus)

When we order up a round,
we disavow six feet of ground,
but rush to gaming, place our bet,
at *this* you'll find us in a sweat.
What goes on here in the pub
amid the coin and chug-a-lug,
be this the scene that you seek out,
it's this that I would speak about.

One and all they drink and game,
they live a life that knows no shame,
those who trust in a gambler's knack
depart the game with a barren back,
some leave the premises very well
  healed,
others leave naked in sack cloth
  concealed.
No one there of death thinks twice
when for the drinks they roll the dice.

First they roll to see who pays —
to that their cups they freely raise;
they drink next to all who captive
  dwell
and third to those alive and well,
fourth to their Christian brethren,
fifth to the dearly departed. Amen!
Sixth to vain sisters as years take their
  toll,
seventh to foresters out on patrol.

Eighth to such brothers as don't
  give a damn,
ninth to the absentees out on the lam,
tenth to sea captains addicted to sailing,
eleventh to rioters, ranting and railing,
twelfth to the rueful who penance pay,
thirteenth to the backpacking émigré,
as much to the papacy as to the king,
they untiringly drink to everything.

Host and hostess unstintingly pour,
there's nothing the parson or soldier
  likes more,
they drink, one and all, irrespective of
  gender,
the table-top wiper and sweetmeat
  vendor.
They drink, the swift and slow of wit,
whether black or white doesn't
  matter a bit,
drink the steadfast and dissipated,
the ignorant and doctorated.

Drinks the poor man in failing health,
prodigal son gone to waste with his
  wealth,
the aging man and pubescent lad
cannot recall how much they've had,
the prelate, deacon, mother and hag,
sisters and brothers are all in the bag.
They drink irrespective of gender or
  years,
they drink till it gurgles inside of their
  ears.

Six hundred cups is a meager amount
for those who long since have lost
  track of the count.
And so they imbibe with no limit
  to set,
as gladly they'd swim in it *sans* regret;
thus decent folk do chew us out,
degrade the indigent devout —
Let those who demean us be
  disgraced,
from the rolls of righteous men
  erased.

TRANSLATION

PART III
The Court of Love

15. *Amor volat undique*
  (Soprano and Chorus of Boys)

Love flies about the world entire
o'ertaken by his own desire.
Young men and women, aware of it,
are joined together, as is fit.

If any maid lack her companion,
lacks she all her heart to gladden,
enclosed, instead, within her breast
she chambers dreaded night's
  bequest.
This fate is the bitterest.

16. *Dies, nox et omnia* (Baritone)

Break of day, dark of night,
the whole world holds me in its spite,
the converse maidens keep
  so pains me that I weep,
  so fills me up with sighs,
with fears beyond disguise.

O my comrades, have your fun,
and mock the likes of one undone,
Ah, pity the wretch that I've become,
  great is my grief,
  bring me relief
by what honor you've won.

The very beauty of your face
makes myriad tears down my cheeks
  race,
no heart, but ice is in its place.
  The remedy
  to rally me,
a kiss, please, by your grace.

17. *Stetit puella* (Soprano)

There stood a girl
  in crimson gowned;
the dress if but touched
  breathed a rustling sound.
Eia!

There stood a girl
  exquisitely posed;
her complexion a flower,
  her mouth red as rose.
Eia!

18. *Circa mea pectora*
  (Baritone and Chorus)

Alas that my heart
with sighs falls apart
in longing for thy beauty —
O how the sighs undo me.

*Manda liet,
manda liet,*
my beloved I call
she comes not at all.

Your eyes dance with light
than the sun's own more bright
like lightning resplendent
that dazzles the night.

May one and all the gods consent
to grant my spirit's fond intent
that she depart my company
unchained from her virginity.

19. *Si puer cum puellula* (Sextet)

If lad and maid slip away
for a moment's bit of play,
happy is their embrace
as passion increasing
puts shame to disgrace.
Then is sport past words to tell,
arms, limbs, and lips and all pell-mell.

20. *Veni, veni, venias* (Double Chorus)

Come, please come, do not delay
else am I undone this day,
*hyrca, hyrce, nazaza
trillirivos . . .*

Face, flawless, fair
exquisite hair
neck, fragrant, bare
all past compare!

JEFFREY M. DUBAN

More rosy than the rose,
no whiter lily grows,
fairer than all the rest,
in you I'm ever blessed!

21. *In trutina* (Soprano)

My mind's twin contrariety
does lay the equal claim to me
of lusty love or chastity.
But what I see, that I select
and to the yoke submit my neck;
let it my every thought direct.

22. *Tempus est iocundum*
(Soprano, Baritone and Chorus)

Dear maidens, the season
now does call.
rejoice young bachelors
one and all.

Oh, oh, oh — I flower from head
  to toe,
now with maidens' love
am I aglow,
new love is this
that lays me low.

I thrill to think his
wish I'll grant,
grieve to consider
that I shan't.

All Winter long
man perseveres,
by Spring his lust
is in arrears.

Virginity
I'd cast away,
but innocence
won't let me stray.

Come joyously
my only one,
come, else am I
this day undone.

23. *Dulcissime* (Soprano)

Boy most sweet
To you I give myself complete!

Blanziflor and Helena

24. *Ave formosissima* (Chorus)

Hail to thee, most beautiful,
  gem, exceeding rare.
Hail, O grace of maidenhood,
  maid beyond compare.
Hail shining light of all the world.
  Hail rose of earth entire,
Blanziflor and Helena
  breath of Spring's desire.

THE LIBRARY
ST. MARY'S COLLEGE OF MARYLAND
ST. MARY'S CITY, MARYLAND 20686